Fishing

Learn from the Tips

& Laugh at the Tales

By

George F Mason

Books by the same author

Fiction

The Fishing Detectives: Carp Rustlers

The Fishing Detectives: Bun In The Oven

Bossyboots

No Fishing In Here: Just Short Stories

Non-fiction

A Staffordshire Boy: Tales of Fishing and Other Fun

Freelance Writing: How to get Started as a Freelance Writer

Self-Publishing Paperbacks: Plus Ebooks on Kindle and Smashwords

Contents

Contents Continued

Great anglers exist
Side by side
One fishes for pleasure
The other to survive

Introduction

I spent over thirty years of my life working in a factory, the money was handy and the banter with my colleagues was most enjoyable, but every day without exception I yearned to be on the riverbank. Eventually, after a period of wishful thinking, the inevitable sword of redundancy swung my way, and I vowed that once I was out of that factory I would never work in another.

With this in mind, I retrained as a freelance writer and now I have been able to achieve one of my life's ambitions, to write a book about angling. The volume you are holding is the result of my endeavours. It has been put together over a number of years and arranged in a way that hopefully you will find helpful and entertaining.

It is essentially a book of two parts. The first is all about passing on tips to improve catch rates and therefore the angling experience. I make no claim to being the originator of any of these tips; some are common sense, while others have been passed down over the years. However, my observations are unique to me, and are used hopefully to verify the validity of each tip.

The second part of the book is all about tales; stories of incidents that happened to me in the real angling world. I am not a celebrity and don't have access to private waters, in fact, I am just a "normal angler" who has had some success in local matches. But fishing isn't all about competitions; I've had some of the best times of my life while taking part in pleasure sessions with good mates for company. I've also spent hundreds of hours in our beautiful countryside and I feel privileged to have witnessed mother-nature doing her stuff. I hope that you can relate to the stories within and expect that many of you will have similar stories to tell, but these are mine and at last I have committed them to paper.

So whether you are a seasoned piscatorial engineer or just a lad who likes to dip his rod now and again, I hope you find the tips in this book useful and most of all, that you enjoy reading it.

Tips Section 1: Bait

I am starting the tips part of this book with a section regarding bait because this is the single most important factor when it comes to catching fish.

You can buy the finest tackle in the world and master all the techniques required of a good angler, but if you can't tempt the fish to put your bait into its mouth you are destined to catch a net full of nothing. Changing floats won't help and neither will moving to another spot. Of course you need appropriate bait, but the most important thing is, it must be so clean that fish can't resist it.

Here are my top ten tips regarding bait.

Tip 1: Bait boxes

Ask yourself one question. Could you eat your cornflakes out of one of your bait boxes? If the answer is no, then they are not clean enough.

Sure I know what it's like on a Sunday after a long session. You were up early, fished your socks off all morning and you're feeling knackered. This is the lowest part of the day and now you have to make a decision. What are you going to do with the bait you have left over? Half a pint of maggots, a handful of pinkies and some sweetcorn, the choice is yours. A small part of you says throw it in the swim, but you don't, and there are two reasons why.

Firstly, there are the rules of the venue; these state that any left-over bait must not be thrown into the water at the end of a session. However, the second and perhaps the real reason for your decision to hang onto your bait is because like most anglers, you're tighter than a chub's bum. Well, we all know pinkies last forever and they'll be all right for next week's session or at least they'll be okay for an evening down the cut one night after work. You promise yourself you'll stick the left over sweetcorn in a plastic bag and pop it into the freezer as soon as you get home. And as for the maggots, you convince yourself that by next Sunday they will have all turned into lovely casters, which will save you having to buy some for next week's session.

The trouble is when you finally arrive home you are so tired from getting up early and so relaxed from the beer you drank in the pub on the way back, that everything goes straight into the shed. You make a beeline for the couch, sleep all afternoon and wake up with the Antiques Roadshow on the telly and to a wife who's got the hump. The last thing on your mind is the bait that you put in the shed earlier.

So when you next get your tackle out, there is a jungle growing out of the box that contained the sweetcorn. The box with the pinkies is worse, it smells of ammonia (maggot piss) and bran is stuck all around the inside like the leaves in a fortune-teller's teacup. Of course you've done this all before and it comes as no surprise to you that the box that held the half pint of maggots is the worst. Yes, some of the contents have turned to casters, but they're not those lovely orange match winning casters that roach can't refuse, these are dark red stinking casters and some of them have hatched, so when you removed the lid half a dozen big hairy bluebottles flew past in a formation that would've done the red arrows proud.

Ah well, you tip the rest of the contents into the bin and your boxes are ready to be filled up again. If you recognise this scenario and you are failing to catch while your mate is bagging up, now you know why. Don't be lazy, clean your bait boxes, you wouldn't want your dinner served on a filthy plate would you?

Quick Tip

If you intend on using bread for bait during a session, do it first, it won't be half as effective once you have introduced some maggots, or other meaty bait. It would be like asking a trucker to turn vegetarian when he's half-way through eating a bacon butty.

Tip 2: Prepare your bait

It follows on that if your bait boxes are clean then your bait should be the same. The majority of anglers that I know acquire their bait on the day before they go fishing. The man in the shop fills up their bait boxes, which are not opened again until the following day when they arrive at the water.

The result is a box of maggots that have been crawling around in bran or maize that has been soaked with their own urine for a long time. The whole of the contents smells foul. Yes, I know what you are thinking; fish hunt for their food by smell, so they will be attracted to something that whiffs a bit. Well they won't. How would you like to eat your sandwiches with a smell that is reminiscent of a public toilet in the height of summer, wafting up your nostrils?

All bait should be fresh and clean, especially maggots which should be washed on the same day, if not at least on the evening before a session.

Yes, I know you've probably read the last paragraph twice, and no, I haven't been sitting in the sun for too long. Wash your maggots is exactly what I said. I know that some anglers have trouble with the concept of washing their hands, so washing maggots is going to be a task of gigantic proportions, but believe me it will be well worth it.

How the hell do you wash a maggot? I hear you cry. Well for those of you who want to claim an advantage over your fishing buddies, who are using filthy bait, please follow these instructions.

Items required for washing your maggots.

A maggot sieve (available from any good tackle shop)

Some fresh bran (available from any pet shop)

Two clean bait boxes (see tip one)

A small glass of water (available from any tap)

The method

(A) Remove lid from bait box, lower head inside and breathe in deeply through the nose. This is just to remind you how putrid these things smell, especially in warm weather.

(B) Sieve the maggots to remove all the old bran, dead maggots, maize and any other detritus that the little wrigglers are scuttling about in.

(C) The maggots should then be placed into a clean bait box.

(D) Now just damp the maggots with a little water and sprinkle with a handful of fresh bran. Give them a shake and the bran will soak up the excess moisture.

(E) Sieve again and put the neat maggots into the second clean bait box, then add a small handful of fresh bran.

(F) Finally, lower your head into the box again and take another long sniff. Yes, I know, they smell so damn good you could eat them yourself.

The same method can be used for pinkies, but for squatts or feeders you will need a different size sieve. These little fellows are much smaller and supplied in foundry sand which doesn't mix well with food, if you've ever had a picnic on a beach you'll know what I mean, just one grain in a sandwich is enough to have you spitting for a week. I don't like sand in my food, so why should fish be any different?

The problem with squatts or feeders is that they and the sand will fall straight through a normal sieve. So what I use is a piece of gauze that can be purchased from any car accessory shop. It's the stuff that is used to support the filler when bodywork has been damaged. It's cheap and easy to bend into a shape suitable for sieving. All you need to do is follow the same method that was used for sieving the maggots and you will soon have a bait ready to attract even the fussiest fish.

Luncheon meat is another bait that often goes to the water totally unprepared. A tin is often thrown into the bottom of the tackle box just in case your favourite bait doesn't have the fish climbing up your rod.

The problem with a tin of luncheon meat is that once it is opened you are faced with a lump of pink meat that needs cutting into cubes. It should also be remembered the cubes need to be the correct size and suit the hook you intend on using. You may also want to cut some smaller ones to offer as loose feed or to mix in with your groundbait.

So with nothing much doing with the other baits that you've been using, you decide to give the meat a bash. You've got to keep one eye on your float, so you have to tackle the luncheon meat half blind. You get a bait box lid to use as a plate and then you attempt to cut the meat to the correct shape with your rusty old penknife. Okay, your efforts would look good if you were a visually challenged chef, but with regards to having produced a bait for catching fish the results are pretty poor. The whole operation has taken ages, the meat is the wrong size and it has probably been dropped on the muddy bank several times. It's also getting warm so it has lost its firmness and is attracting a swarm of flies.

Given this scenario, wouldn't it have been better if you had opened the tin the night before while you were in the luxury of your own kitchen. Using a plate to rest it on, you could have sliced the meat with one of those super-sharp knives that your wife paid a fortune for. It could have been cut up to perfection without any fuss. You could have put some cling film over it and popped it into the fridge and the next morning it would be cool, firm and ready to catch any fish with carnivorous tendencies.

If you do as I have suggested, with your luncheon meat, you will also find that you are more likely to use it. This is because you won't have to go through the hassle of opening a tin on the bank, which means you won't have to sit without a bite for another hour under the false assumption that a fish will take your sweetcorn soon. You will also find that, because the meat has been in the fridge all night, it will be less likely to fly off the hook when you make a long cast to that distant reed bed where all the big fish are hiding.

So the moral of the story is this. No matter what bait you are going to use, make sure it is clean, fresh and well prepared. Smelly and stale just won't do, that is unless you don't like getting your nets wet.

Tip 3: Fresh please

Do not be tempted to use frozen sweetcorn. Yes I know that there are hundreds of you out there who don't believe in using it as bait anyway. As a friend of mine who lives up north and sounds like Peter Kay once said to me, "If I have to resort to putting a piece of sweetcorn on me hook, that's the day I'll likely as not pack up fishing altogether."

But there are thousands of anglers who use it all the time, and with good reason. It's cheap, convenient to buy, can be kept in the tin for ages. It stays on the hook, is easy to loose feed and last but not least, most fish love it.

Anyway, the thing is, you must buy it in tins. Yes, I know it's cheaper to buy a big sack of the frozen stuff and it tastes nice with the roast pork on a Sunday, but as a bait it is a poor substitute for its tinned counterpart. The trouble with frozen sweetcorn is that it hasn't got the same attractive smell as the other variety. The only way a fish can find frozen sweetcorn is by seeing it and as you know most of our fisheries do not contain clear water, in fact, most fish would have a job to see one of their own fins in front of their faces. So it's clear that if the fish are going to locate your bait they will have to do it by using their powers of smell.

I'd had this theory about sweetcorn for some time but real proof came to me during a fishing trip with my friend Tom. It was an early morning session, on a lovely day in late June. We were fishing a small pool that extended to about two acres with an average depth of about six feet or two metres if you prefer it in metric. Although it is fringed all around with reeds the rest of the water is quite featureless. The bottom is level and covered with dark, fine silt. There are only a small number of pegs dotted around the water and these are restricted to several small wooden jetties. They all protrude out from the reed bed, and it was one of these that Tom and I shared on the morning in question.

The venue is renowned for its large population of tench and it was this species that we set out to catch. We both set up the same, size fourteen hooks, waggler floats and of course we both chose the same bait. In fact, we were so alike you'd think we'd invented a new sport called synchronised fishing. We both loose fed a few offerings about three rod lengths out and both had sweetcorn on our hooks.

I was soon into my first fish, a tench of a couple of pounds and this set the pattern for the rest of the morning, in fact, I had twenty five more tench all of a similar size and several roach that were big enough to warrant the landing net. Tom, however, whose float was getting ever closer to mine, finished the day with only three tench and a net full of envy. He was pig sick every time he saw me bending into another one. He copied my depth, shotting pattern and everything else, the only difference and I'm sure you are ahead of me already, was that he was using frozen sweetcorn.

Tip 4: Additives

Here is a topic that could be the subject for a whole book. However, my take on additives is as follows.

We already know that fish use their sense of smell to find their food, so they will be attracted by certain smells just like we are. Nothing arouses my appetite faster than the aroma of a hot dog blowing in the wind. It's the smell of sausage and onions mixed with a very large portion of fresh air that makes it so appealing. If you could only smell the hot dog, you'd probably be put off for life.

The secret is in the concentration. If you are going to use an additive, do it sparingly, this is definitely a case where less is more. I can recall fishing a big national match on the river Witham in Lincolnshire during the mid-nineties. I was part of a five-man team and we had a plan to go all out for eels straight from the start. We also had a secret weapon, three bottles of an additive, each one of which was supposed to contain the delicious concentrated juices of about a million worms. We thought that this would drag in the eels from miles around and we'd all bag up.

Because it was a team match, we got our bait as a job lot; a gallon of maggots, half a gallon of pinkies and two pints of squatts. After the draw the bait was dished out and one of the team, Tim, was responsible for putting a couple of drops of the additive into each of the angler's bait boxes along with their bait. Now Tim was a jolly good fellow and one that could never be accused of being slow when it came to exploiting an opportunity. He only used two bottles of the additive during the process of dishing it out, which meant he had a bottle left over. Now instead of putting a few drops on his bait like he had for the rest of the team, he went a bit rash and used the whole bottle.

His thinking was simple; the more of the stuff he put on his bait, the more eels he'd catch. He would win the match, loads of money and be the hero of our fishing club. The reality, as it turned out, was completely different. He was the only man in our team who had a dry net and he recorded nil points. He couldn't even put it down to a bad draw as the anglers either side of him both did better than average in their section. We ribbed him about his performance during the trip back home and this was when he confessed to what he had done. He was now convinced that he'd have been better off with no additive rather than having too much.

Whether certain additives or exotic smells can increase an angler's catch rate is often the focus of debate. Each angler has their favourite or they don't believe in them at all. Boilies are an example and have been flavoured with every concoction under the sun. For my part I can't believe they all work, but I am equally sure that some do. I don't know how it would be possible to find out which ones work and which don't, after all if you try a new one and have a good day, how do you know that you wouldn't have had just as good a day without it. The opposite is also true, you could use a fantastic additive that fails on a day when nothing on earth would get you a bite.

Having said all that, I think a lot of it is down to confidence. During the eighties I won my fishing club's annual championship for two years in succession. To be successful I had to do well in a series of matches that were held throughout the year, so winning the annual trophy twice showed that, if nothing else, I was at least consistent. During this time, I came across an additive called "red cap," it was also known as "the Sharneyford secret" and I used this in all my matches. It smelt of bubble gum and could be detected by the anglers on the next few pegs down-wind of me. This led them to believe that I had a secret ingredient, which of course I did, but I never let on what it was. You couldn't get it in our local tackle shop I had to buy it from a dealer, who was sixty-miles away, when I was visiting my first wife's family.

Anyway, whether or not this stuff helped to attract fish I'm not absolutely sure, but it definitely didn't seem to put any off and it raised my confidence no end. My winning ways could just have easily been down to using clean bait, but we'll never know because for some reason red cap became unavailable.

Quick Tip

Match your hook size to the bait you are using, not to the fish you are hoping to catch. If you change baits don't be too lazy to change your hook, nothing looks dafter and is less likely to catch fish than a single caster on a size ten.

Match your hook to your bait not the fish

right   *silly*

Tip 5: New baits

Every now and again a new bait comes into the angling news. I can still remember the excitement that came with the discovery that river Severn barbel couldn't get enough luncheon meat. Until then most anglers used bread, worms or maggots, but now meat is a common bait used for a lot of species. Sweetcorn is another phenomena that fits into the same bracket along with pellets and dog biscuits.

The point of all this is that, very often, when an angler is thinking of trying out a new bait, he does it half-heartedly. He will go to the venue armed with his tried and tested array of baits just in case the new one doesn't work. When he begins fishing, instead of trying out the new bait first, he starts off with his usual bait and will carry on fishing with it just as long as he is catching some fish. However, as we all know, bites peter out at some point in the day and it is this that sparks the angler into having a go with the new bait. The results are disappointing; it doesn't work because the fish are full to bursting and having a kip in the nearest weed bed. The angler meanwhile, thinks the new bait is a waste of space and next time he only takes his usual with him.

There is a lesson to be learnt here, and that is once the fish have gone off the feed, they will stay off the feed regardless of what juicy morsels the angler decides to throw at them. So, if you've heard about a new bait or invented one yourself that you think will be a fish slayer, do the right thing and give it a bash as soon as you get to the water, not after your swim has died.

Tip 6: Feeding patterns

Feeding little and often, is one of the truest bits of fishing wisdom that has ever been passed on, but some anglers choose to ignore it. I learned the lesson early in my fishing career and I've never forgotten it.

It was a perfect June morning and I arrived at the pool at about five o'clock. The mist still hung low and the water was as calm as a millpond. I quickly set up with a light waggler and was looking forward to a good morning's sport.

The venue was filling up quickly as more anglers arrived and, I suppose that by the time I'd actually started fishing, over half the pegs were taken. The main species of fish in the water were skimmer bream, plus a good head of roach, a few perch and a small number of tench, but not enough to have a crack at. So it was the skimmer bream that I set my stall out for. I introduced a marble size ball of groundbait about three rod lengths out then cast in over it with some punched bread. I'd caught a dozen fish in the first ten minutes and all was well until another angler set up on the peg next to me.

To be honest, when I saw him get a big bowl out of his basket, I thought he'd brought the washing up with him. Actually, it would have been better for me if he had. Anyway, he used the bowl to mix an enormous amount of groundbait, which he fashioned into spheres, each one being about the size of a grapefruit. He then launched a barrage of these missiles into the water as if he was trying to recreate the sinking of the Bismark. The net result of this activity was that I failed to catch any more fish that morning. I don't think it was just the sudden bombardment that stopped me catching; it was also due to the sheer quantity of food that Bomber Harris put into the water.

Now I'm no expert when it comes to statistics, but it seems to me that a rough formula should be followed when introducing groundbait or loose offerings into your swim. I firmly believe that there is an instinct at work here and those who have a natural feel for it, are likely to catch more fish.

Fishing is all about trying to catch as many fish as possible, but if you want to be successful you need to think like a gambler. First you have to choose which bait is going to be the best bet, but that is only the start of the decision making process that all anglers face every time they go fishing. The hard part is deciding how much groundbait or loose offerings to put into your swim at the beginning of a session. This would of course be a lot easier if you knew how many fish were in the vicinity of your hook bait, you could then feed accordingly but that wouldn't half make our sport boring.

If you do as the angler I've mentioned did and fill your swim in with a barrow load of groundbait, you are reducing the odds of a fish picking up the one piece of bait with your hook in it. Even if there is a large shoal of fish in your peg they would soon gorge themselves and then swim off satisfied. On the other hand, if you are too tentative and only put in a small amount of free offerings a few fish could quickly devour these and move on to pastures new. The answer is in the middle ground. Starting off slowly is the best way; always remember that if you make the wrong decision and put too much in, you can't take it out.

Put a small amount of loose feed or groundbait into your swim and then see how long it takes before the first fish comes. If you catch the first quickly add some more free offerings to keep them interested. If you are lucky they might shout to their mates and get them to come over and join in.

If you have ever fed seagulls at the seaside, or ducks in the park, you will know what I mean and this is precisely the behaviour you want your fish to adopt. If you keep catching, keep feeding little and often, keep them keen so that they are fighting for every piece of bait that goes into the water. If the bites start to slow down decrease the loose feed accordingly, do not think that putting more bait into the water will help, it won't.

It's difficult to explain about the feed rate but it forms the basis of the difference between a good angler and a poor angler. I like to think about it in the same way a poker player would, quite simply, you have to think about the odds. If you catapult ten maggots into your swim and there is only one fish in the vicinity the odds that he will take your hook bait first are ten to one. These are not good odds; it does of course get better if there are two fish in your swim the odds then improve to five to one and so on. It's a simple equation; the more bait you put in the lower your chances are of getting a bite. So before you add more and more loose offerings, ask yourself how many fish do you think are in your swim? I know you haven't got a crystal ball and you can't see through the water but it is possible to build up an idea.

The number of fish in your swim, the amount of loose feed put in and the frequency at which you get a bite, all depend on each other. I can't stress enough the need to think about this all the time when you are fishing. Ask yourself this question. If during the last half-hour you've catapulted dozens of maggots into your swim on a regular basis and only had two bites, will another pouch full improve your chances? I think not.

Of course it wouldn't do to go too far the other way, if the fish are in a ravenous mood and you have attracted lots of them into your swim you will need to keep them interested by adopting a regular feeding pattern or they will soon move on. The secret is to keep the bait going in little and often. If you are catching well, don't increase the amount of feed you are putting in, it is much better to reduce the interval between feeds. Try to keep this consistent while you are catching steadily and the fish will stay with you. If the bites slow down, just increase the length of time between feeds.

During a session you can expect activity to fluctuate because fish are easily spooked. Perhaps seeing one of their mates struggling might put them off for a little while or they might be scattered by a passing pike. Just remember, whatever happens, don't pile the bait in because little and often is generally the best way. Use the frequency of bites to regulate the time interval between feeds. You will end up getting a sixth sense about this and then you will see your catch rate improve.

Tip 7: Plumbing the depth

This is one area where the match angler reigns supreme. He knows that if he is fishing at the wrong depth it will cost him dearly. It's quite simple, if you want to catch fish you need to present your bait at the correct depth and if you don't know with some accuracy what that depth is; your catch rate is going to be much lower than it could be.

It's also worth remembering that knowing how deep your swim is will not only help with your bait presentation it will also improve your bite detection.

Presentation

Just imagine you arrive at a pool that you are unfamiliar with. You choose a peg that looks like it might be productive. The wind is in the right direction; that is blowing from behind so that you can take advantage of the calm water. Yes, I know that the experts say you should always fish with the wind in your face, but what the hell, if you can't fish in comfort what's the point. Anyway, as you put your tackle down a fish jumps about two rod lengths out and this urges you to set up as fast as possible, there is no time to lose because the catch of a lifetime could be about to get away.

Before you know it you are sticking your float on the line and, because you are so eager to get your bait out there, you take a wild guess at the depth. You glance at the water and reckon it's about six feet deep, so that'll do. You tie on your hook quickly and put your shot on the line with equal speed, after all you know how much shot this float takes because you use it week in week out, despite having a box full that have never even touched water.

Anyway, you cast in, add some groundbait or loose feed then sit back full of anticipation. If you don't get a bite in ten minutes you reel in and check that your sweetcorn hasn't fallen off your hook. Then you cast out again and add some more free offerings.

At the opposite end, under the water that just happens to be about twelve feet deep, a nice shoal of bream and a few tench are feeding ravenously on the free offerings that you've put in. Their tails are in the air and they are quite oblivious to your hook bait, which is swinging about like a church bell, well out of reach.

After another twenty biteless minutes you reel in and decide to have a change of bait. In fact during the first hour you make lots of changes but the situation doesn't improve until you plumb the depth properly. You are surprised at how far out your estimate was, but now you cast out with renewed optimism and you start to catch. What a waste of an hour when it would've taken about two minutes to do it right in the first place.

Bite detection

Just imagine the opposite scenario; in your hurry to set up, you set your depth much too deep. Well how were you supposed to know this was the shallow end of the lake? You guessed at six foot just like you always do, but in reality it's only two feet deep.

You reel in after not having a bite for a while to find your bait has gone and you assume it fell off when you cast out, but in reality a clever fish had it without even registering the slightest tremor on your float. Well, perhaps the fish wasn't that clever, it didn't have to be really, not with you having four foot of spare line strung across the bottom of the pool.

So when you are setting up, take a deep breath and plumb the depth thoroughly. And when I say that, I mean check the depth for quite a way out. Not all waters start out shallow at the side and get deeper as you go further out. Some do the opposite and others have all sorts of troughs, ledges and gullies in them.

Talking of ledges and gullies this is generally where the majority of fish hang out. So when you explore the depth, don't just decide to fish at five rod lengths because on a good day that's how far you can cast, search for the ledges and you will find the fish.

So always plumb the depth, if your bait isn't where a fish can find it, you'll catch much less than you could, it's as simple as that.

Quick Tip

In the autumn months pick some elderberries when they are just ripening. They should be a dark maroon colour and you need to get them before they go soft. Try using them on the hook when feeding hemp seed. They are lighter on the hook than hemp so presentation is improved and fish love them.

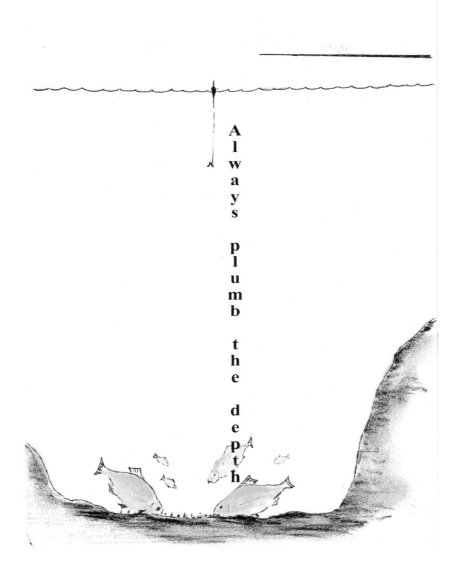

Always plumb the depth

Tip 8: Feed first

It always surprises me just how many anglers get this wrong. They will cast out to their chosen spot put the rod onto their rod rest and then catapult or throw in some loose offerings using their float as the target.

I'm not suggesting for a minute that you won't catch fish this way but it isn't the best way. Here is what you should do. I'm assuming you've plumbed the depth and have found a ledge about four and half rod lengths out. Put in some loose feed and then quickly cast over it so that your hook bait is sinking just behind the loose offerings. The fish in your swim will quickly mop these up (that is assuming that you are feeding little and often) and will then take your hook bait.

I once fished a match on the Leeds-Liverpool canal on the outskirts of Liverpool. The water there was almost as clear as a mountain stream and it gave me a real insight into fish behaviour. Apparently, the water was so clear because, during the seventies and eighties, very few pleasure boats used the canal in that part of the world. I wasn't expecting this and couldn't think of a new plan so I started the day with the usual method I used on canals that were new to me. This involved a small pinch of squats, which I would loose feed just over the near shelf and I would then follow in quickly with a single pinkie on a size twenty. After repeating this process several times, I noticed that a shoal of small fish kept coming up towards the surface; they would intercept the loose fed squatts then disappear again.

They re-appeared each time I threw in a few loose offerings. They waited patiently in the depths, but as soon as the squatts fell onto the surface of the water, they were up again and devoured the loose offerings as if they hadn't eaten for a week.

When I first saw this phenomena, I got quite excited, they were only small perch weighing no more than a couple of ounces a piece, but they would soon make a good weight if I could take a few while the going was good. I thought it would be easy to catch these fish but even though I followed the advice already given to drop the hook bait in straight after the loose feed I still didn't catch. These fish simply ignored my hook bait even though I was careful to get it in with the loose feed.

The answer of course was that these fish were used to the clear water and were able to judge the speed at which my bait descended. Fish might not be clever but they, like most animals, have an acute sense of instinct and, in this case, it was telling them that the pinkie was different from the rest of the stuff they were eating. So, being pretty bright myself, I decided to reduce my hook to a size twenty-two and change my bait to a single squatt. This change brought me a couple of fish but they were soon ignoring my hook bait again because it was dropping through the water faster than the loose feed. The answer was simple; I moved my bottom shot up to the bottom of the float.

Bingo, the very next chuck in I hooked another. This was just as well as I was beginning to pull my hair out by now. But my success didn't last long. I caught two more and although they were still mopping up the loose feed they ignored my hook bait again. The only other thing I could do was change down to an even smaller hook. I didn't think I'd ever use the twenty sixes I'd purchased some while ago, but if there was ever an occasion to try them this was it. Like the change before, it worked for a while and I managed to catch a few more fish before the most frustrating match I'd ever fished came to an end. I weighed in 1lb 8oz and with that managed to take third prize.

The locals chuckled when I told them how lucky they were that I hadn't caught all the fish in my swim. The reason for their laughter was, apparently, that these fish are visible in most pegs, but are so difficult to catch that the locals ignore them. They all preferred to fish well over hoping for a tench or some of the nice roach that reside just under the far shelf.

I may have come third and won a small amount of pools money on that day, but for me, the most important thing was seeing how those fish responded to loose feed. I know the water was clear and that they modified their behaviour, but one thing was for sure, if I'd used the tactic of casting first and then feeding my float I'd have almost certainly finished with a dry net.

Tip 9: Traditional baits

If Izaak Walton could see what anglers are putting on their hooks now, he'd have a fit. Gone are the days when an angler would have a good day's sport armed with only a jar of worms and a crust of bread.

Today's fisherman is spoilt for choice, not only is he able to buy a range of maggots to suit every occasion but also a mind boggling plethora of other foods, that apparently, fish will find irresistible.

I have just visited a bait supplier to find out what you can buy and here are just a few examples of the hundreds of items now available.

Pellets of every shape size and flavour

Boilies in a variety of flavours

Garlic hemp seed

Naked oats

Frenzied cat meat

Tiger nuts (No wonder tigers are dying out)

Basically the average angler is spoilt for choice; every item comes in a complete range of colours and flavours. They are all guaranteed to drive fish into a feeding frenzy and if one doesn't work then next week you can try something else. By the time you've done all the permeations, you'll be collecting your pension.

Perhaps it is time to take stock, go back to basics and have a go with some of the old tried and trusted baits. After all, I doubt that fish have changed their palates as fast as the bait manufacturers have extended their lines. Here is a suggestion, have a fishing session without the weird or exotic, leave the pineapple flavoured maize at home and try one of these traditional baits.

Cheese

A lump of cheddar is easy to buy and use. Just mould it onto your hook and expect a good response from fish like carp, roach and chub.

Bread flake

Buy a loaf of bread (not sliced) pick a small piece off and pinch it onto your hook. This is irresistible to most fish especially bream, carp, tench and roach.

Worms

Very underrated, fish just love them and are taken by most species. If you are after big perch this bait takes some beating.

Slugs

If you are a gardener, this is a win win situation, go out on any damp night in the summer and your garden will be teaming with the little blighters. Likely as not, the vile creatures will be chewing the heads off your prize hostas. Here's your opportunity to take revenge, bang one on the hook and get ready for a monster chub to devour it.

Wasp grubs

I hate wasps, so do yourself and the rest of the civilised world a favour, dig up as many nests as you can and enjoy some fantastic sport.

Cheese comes to the rescue

One of my favourite methods of fishing is with a stick float on a good river. Unfortunately there are no decent sized rivers close to where I live, so to indulge in a bit of good stick float fishing I have to travel about fifty miles to the river Trent in Derbyshire.

Yes, I can hear some of you scoffing, but others will remember how good it was in the seventies and eighties. Every week-end would see both banks lined with anglers all the way from Shardlow to the Humber estuary. And it was in the eighties that I found myself heading towards that river with Eddy, one of my pals. We worked in the same factory and had taken a day off to go fishing. The sad thing was it had rained all night and although we were feeling optimistic we also knew that when we arrived the river might be un-fishable.

In reality, when we arrived at Long Eaton it was worse than we expected. We should have turned around and gone straight home, but we had the bait, where could we use half a gallon of maggots in our neck of the woods? And there was the hemp seed, that I spent an hour cooking secretly in my wife's best saucepan while she was down the women's institute talking about jam.

"Come on we might as well give it a go now that we are here," said Eddy, "I can't face the long trek back to the car park just yet and they might be biting like mad."

If there was any madness about, it belonged to us and not the fish. For two hours we trotted our floats down the swollen river and all we had to show for it was a gudgeon each. Still, they say that every cloud has a silvery lining and we had at least managed to use some of our bait.

We'd been going through the routine of saying we'd pack up soon, when we decided that, instead of going home, we'd try our luck at a lake in Nottinghamshire. This water was getting some good revues and, as we'd already come fifty miles, another twenty wouldn't make much difference. Having decided that this was a good idea we packed up pretty quickly, not just in anticipation of bagging some of the bream that the venue was known for, but because the bailiff hadn't arrived yet to take our day ticket money.

Three quarters of an hour later we were setting up on the lake. Big wagglers and big smiles, it looked good.

Looked good was as good as it got. You need to feed heavy was the tip in the angling press so we showered the place with maggots trying to attract one of the big shoals of bream. It might have been better if we'd had some groundbait, but we had intended on fishing the river so we hadn't taken any with us.

Another two hours soon passed by and our anticipation and excitement turned into depression. We hadn't had so much as a knock between us. It had all been a waste of a day off work and a waste of money spent on bait and petrol.

"Come on let's pack up and go home," said Eddy, "if we are quick, we can get away before the bailiff arrives, at least we can save money on another day ticket."

Neither of us wanted to spend money if we could get away with it, so we threw what was left of our bait into the water and packed our tackle away quicker than ever. On the way back to the car park, Eddy even took a short cut through a bramble hedge just in case the person heading in our direction along the bank was the bailiff coming to collect our money.

I guess you could be wondering now where this tale is heading, but please be patient and I will put you out of your misery.

On the way home I made a comment to Eddy, that we'd have been better off fishing the local mill pool.

"Let's go there now," he said, excitedly. "It's only just after lunch we've got most of the afternoon left."

"Yeah, I would love to, if only we hadn't thrown what was left of our bait into the lake," I replied, and saw the look of despondency come across his face.

"I'm not wasting any more money on maggots," he said, sadly.

This was when I remembered fishing the mill pool years ago and watching an old man being very successful with cheese.

Anyway, Eddy agreed to part with fifty pence and I went into the village shop and bought half a pound of cheddar. It was armed with just this bait that we set up at the mill pool.

No float this time, it was just a small bomb about eighteen inches from a size ten hook onto which a lump of cheese was moulded, just enough to cover the hook without masking the point.

There was always a big raft of flotsam at the calm end of the mill pool and it was just upstream of this that we cast our baits. We then put our rods into their rests and sat back to await developments. It wasn't long before we were both rewarded as, almost in unison, the tops of our rods bent round and we were both playing good chub around the three-pound mark. There wasn't even any need to strike either, as the fish virtually hooked themselves.

This was repeated several times before the chub became suspicious and refused to play any more. But by then we'd both had some nice fish, some of which were pushing the four-pound barrier, which isn't bad for small river chub.

I guess the moral is simple. We'd spent a lot of time and money on bait and we'd chased fish over three counties, but in the end we finished up having some great sport, four miles from home with a lump of cheddar cheese.

So next time you are filling up your tackle box with cat food, dog biscuits and chillie-con-carne flavoured maple peas. Ask yourself if you'd be better off with half a loaf and a bit of cheddar.

Tip 10: Commit yourself

Repetition definitely improves any skill and this is especially true when it comes to fishing. But don't worry I'm not about to start giving you advice regarding technique; you will be able to find that elsewhere. What I am talking about here is having one or several sessions where you have totally committed yourself to a new bait.

Most anglers assume that if you can catch fish with one type of bait then you can fish with anything; it's just a matter of changing the bait on the hook. This is further than a country mile from the truth. It's like expecting a musician to pick up any instrument and play it. Yes, I'm sure he'd be better than a non-musician but it would still take him time to master it completely. And that's what fishermen who want to catch more fish should strive to do. It's no good going out with your favourite bait and method and dabbling with something new ten minutes before you pack up to go home. If you want to master it, then you must go for it whole hog, like a pig that's found a potato.

Hemp Seed

Hemp is one of those baits that few people manage to use to its full potential. Sure, I know a lot of anglers take some with them every time they go on a session and use it for loose feed, but how many use it on their hooks?

Most anglers throw hemp seed into the water just because they have heard it is good for attracting fish. They wouldn't think of putting it on their hook, and if they did it would only be for a minute before they went back to the caster or maggot. How about going out fishing one day with just a bag of hemp, and while you're at it, why not go all the way and make it a bag of hemp that you've prepared yourself, not one of those ready cooked bags that has been hanging about in the tackle shop for weeks.

You will learn about the best float to use, the way the fish takes the bait, which happens to be pretty damn quick, and how to put the stuff on the hook so that it doesn't mask the point or come off during casting.

I know one angler who was so convinced that hemp seed was a magic bait, that when it came to his annual holidays he spent a week fishing with nothing but hemp. Okay, so his wife divorced him because she was looking forward to a week in the Algarve, but he did go on to win lots of money and trophies.

Punched Bread

Punched bread is another bait that requires the full commitment of the angler if he's to reap the full benefits of this great bait.

Real finesse is required here, fine tackle and a float that will hit the water as light as an angel's kiss, yet be ready to register a bite the moment the hook bait touches the surface. Punched bread fishing is all about putting a pellet of bread into the water after feeding a fine groundbait with particles so small they will attract the fish without giving them much to actually feed on.

Fish are often caught in the mid to upper layers of the water, where they are more transient and easily spooked. This means the angler needs to have a light touch and keep any disturbance to the absolute minimum.

Anglers who hear about the successes achieved by those using punched bread, especially on canals, often give it a quick whirl but then, quite wrongly, dismiss it as a waste of time. They turn up at the side of the cut and use the same set up they would use for gudgeon bashing and can't understand why they aren't catching. The reason they don't succeed is because their tackle has been designed to get their bait down to the bottom as quickly as possible where their target fish feed. Punched bread fishing is an art and like so many other methods it will improve your catch rate if you fully commit to it. Why not just take a loaf, some fine breadcrumb and a bread punch with you next time you go out and see what this method is capable of.

Quick tip

When fishing with punched bread I often find that feeding a marble size ball of fine feed, just before the hook bait, is enough to keep the fish interested. However, on some waters especially canals that are not too coloured, the fine cloud that is produced by the feed can scare the fish because it looks unnatural to them.

To get over this, I mix a little fine soil in with the fine breadcrumb just to take the edge off it. You obviously need to make sure there are no bits of stone or pebbles in it because you are trying to catch the fish not depth charge them. Mole hill soil is perfect, for some reason it is always fine and contains few stones, so if you know somebody with moles in their lawn, pop round and ask them if you can fill a bucket or two.

Tips Section 2: Tackle

Now that we have sorted out all of the important issues regarding bait, let's move onto the next most important topic, tackle. Here are my top tips and observations; I couldn't arrange them into any sort of importance so I thought I'd start at the sharp end.

Tip 1: Hooks

Yes, I know most of you have probably been using barbless hooks for twenty years and that most waters insist on anglers using them. But there are some people who take a lot more convincing, so here are the benefits again for those who think that if they use barbless hooks they will lose fish.

It's a fact that barbless hooks provide better penetration, they go through the hard part of a fish's mouth much easier than the barbed type. Maggots don't burst, lose all their juices and worms don't rip when they are being put onto a hook with no dreaded barb.

Lastly, and most importantly, I am visiting this well-worn issue for the sake of the fish. I can remember the bad old days and how difficult it was to remove a hook from a fish, especially one that had been hooked deeper than usual. Thankfully now, even if a fish has swallowed the hook further than you would like, removing a barbless hook is so easy the fish doesn't even know about it. Anything that makes sure that the fish doesn't suffer when being caught is a good enough reason for me never to use a hook with a barb again. If you've still got some lurking about in the bottom of your tackle box, why not bite the bullet and sling them now, you know it makes sense.

The other attribute that should be considered when buying hooks, is the length of the shank. Some anglers will go into a shop and ask for hooks by size only, they don't bother to consider the length of the shank, and this is a mistake. Always buy hooks with the longest shanks you can find, and if you find some good ones that suit you, buy plenty because manufacturers have a way of deleting some product lines. This happened to me and the hooks I always swore by are no longer available.

The most important attribute of a long shank hook is more leverage, which gives more control to the angler. The point of control is very small and happens to be where the line meets the hook. The closer to the bend this point is, the less control the angler will have over successfully hooking and getting a fish to the net.

Just imagine a hook that is the shape of a letter u, how much control and leverage would you get with this when compared to a hook that is the same shape as the letter j.

Quick tip

When you are tying your hooks make sure the line comes off the hook at the front of the spade, this will also help with control and leverage.

Tip 2: Line

Fishing line is another area that has changed in the last few years. There was a time when the angler went into a tackle shop and bought his line just by the breaking strain and its length.

"I'll have 50 yards of 10 pound breaking strain please," was all he had to say and perhaps a particular brand name if he had a preference.

Now life has been made more difficult as the angler has to weigh up a lot more information. Every manufacturer is trying to blind them with technology and describing their products with attributes that should be a given. Line is more often bought now by the diameter not the breaking strain, but here are some other descriptions that I've seen used.

Low memory:

Does it keep forgetting it is fishing line?

Abrasion resilient:

Who's rubbing their line and with what?

High knot strength:

What? Any line that can't be knotted without fear of breaking is about as much use as a lead float.

These things may be important to some anglers but what they should be more concerned about is the lines ability to stretch. Line needs a certain amount of give, because without it you would suffer regular break offs. Yes, I know the rod is supposed to be the shock absorber, it is, but it's an extremely crude one.

The rule to follow is, the closer you are fishing, the more stretch you should have in your line. It's just a matter of trying to take a bit of the ferocity out of your strike. This isn't required if you are fishing at a distance, because there will be other factors such as a bow in your line caused by the current or the wind that will make up for the lack of stretch.

Most of my fishing is done at close quarters and I have to admit that I have been guilty of using line that didn't have enough stretch for the type of fishing I was doing.

Perhaps you will recognise this scenario, because before I took notice of the line stretching rule, this happened to me and left me a little red in the face.

I was sitting at the side of the water between a couple of friends and we were all enjoying a bit of good banter and some equally good sport. During this session I struck into a fish in my usual style, but after feeling a heavy contact my line snapped. At this point, I did what every angler does under those circumstances and uttered a few oaths out loud and added words that went something like the following.

"Bloody hell that was a clonker, and the bastard's smashed me."

I'm sure this has happened to you on more than one occasion. Anyway, as I put the rod down I could see my float, and there was a bit of my broken line drifting on top of the water in the margin. Without the slightest thought for my own safety, I decided to try and grab the line in a desperate hope that the clonker of all clonkers might still be attached.

I took a step forward out into the pool, so that I could reach the line, and uttered some more oaths as water flooded in over the top of one of my wellies. But I didn't care because I'd got it, the end of the line was firmly in my hands and the first signs were good, I could feel movement so I quickly began hauling it in. My fishing buddies were watching me now and one of them was getting up with his landing net in his hand preparing to net the clonker. You can always rely on another angler to help you out when you are in dire straights.

As I recovered more line and the fish got closer, I realised that I had made a big mistake. The fish on the hook was a tiddler, a roach actually, about the same size as a gold fish.

"What happened to the bloody clonker?" asked he with the landing net at the ready.

"I don't know," I replied, as I studied the fish, "perhaps a pike had grabbed a hold of him just as I struck and then he let go." It' a shame that there weren't any teeth marks on the roach to back up my theory.

"Your trouble is," says the font of all knowledge, who had remained seated while the drama unfolded, "you strike too hard, I've watched you. As soon as you see your float go under, you go off like a bloody rat trap."

I tried explaining to him as I tipped the water out of my welly, that I struck like that because I had lightening fast reflexes and it was hard to slow them down. It was a curse I'd just have to live with.

"Well if I was you I'd get some line with some more stretch in it, that'll take the sting out."

Now I'm not slow to catch on, I considered what my friend had said and bought some line that was reputed to have plenty of stretch. I can say that it was a success because the number of times that I now break my line when striking has reduced to almost zero.

So, when it comes to line, consider what type of fishing you do and decide if you need line with plenty of stretch or not.

Tip 3: Floats

They say that floats catch more anglers than fish and I think that they are right. Are you one of those anglers who go into the tackle shop on Saturday to buy some bait and while you are waiting for somebody else to be served, you browse the vast array of tackle on offer? You dismiss the rods, reels and that type of stuff because you've already got these big items and you don't really want to part with a big lump of cash. Then your eyes drop onto the floats, and you start to drool. Oh look at all those pretty fellows, every size shape and colour. Some with a fat bobble in the middle, some with a fat bobble at the top. There are small floats for the pole with dainty eyes, and great big pike bungs that look like something that should be bobbing on the sea. There are stick floats made of plastic, balsa, cane or even lignum vitea, and wagglers, short, long, loaded and unloaded.

You pick a few up, look at them tentatively, you read the side to see the shot carrying capacity and imagine it going under. Finally just as the man in front has finished being served you make your choice and with a cavalier attitude you toss the float on the counter and order your bait. Yes, that'll be just the right float for tomorrow you say to yourself and when you get home you put it into your tackle box.

The next day of course, when it comes to fishing, you ignore the new float and the thirty or so other unused floats you've bought in the last twelve months. You are looking for your favourite, the one you always use. Well why not, you like this float, you know how much shot it takes and how it reacts in the wind.

If you are struck down with this affliction that compels you to buy a new float every week, don't despair, you can cure the problem easily by making your own. If you are a pole angler, or a river man, you might still find this chapter interesting, but you will have to carry on buying your own floats. However, if wagglers are your game, I can show you how to make some serious floats and you may never feel the need to buy one ever again.

To make your own wagglers you will need.

Some sarkandas reed or good sized quills

Thick wire

Cocktail sticks

Araldite Rapide

A roll of Solder (can be purchased from DIY shops)

Paint

A little bit of patience

The method

I suggest you make one float first to see how you get on; then make a batch of various lengths and with a variety of shot carrying capacities.

1 Cut the quill or reed to length

2 Take a piece of the wire about 75mm (3 inches) long and on one end make a small loop just a little larger than the diameter of the wire.

3 Mix a small batch of araldite and coat half of the straight end of the wire. This should then be inserted

into the quill or reed leaving the loop and about 25mm (1 inch) of wire sticking out.

4 Before the araldite goes hard, coat 25mm of one of the cocktail sticks and insert this into the other end of the quill. Then put the quill aside to allow the glue to dry. This should take about 20 minutes.

5 When the glue is dry, take another piece of wire and again fashion a loop at one end the same size as the previous one, but before finally closing it, loop it through the one on the bottom of the float. Trim the end to about 8mm, enough for two float rubbers. I always use two because rubber is funny stuff and you never know when it's going to split.

6 To load the float, take some solder and wrap it around the wire sticking out of the bottom of the float. Start at the stem of the float and work neatly downwards towards the loop.

7 Now put the float into a bucket of water and see how it sits. If it sinks altogether remove some of the solder, if it sits too high wrap some more solder around it afresh, and try again. This is where you need the patience if you are going to get it right. I find that by aiming to have most of the float under water leaving just the cocktail stick showing, by the time some more araldite and paint have been added it should be just about right.

8 How low you want it to sit in the water is down to your own personal choice. If you want your bait to descend quickly then adjust the amount of solder so that the float sits higher, you can then add a lot of weight to your line. If on the other hand you are hoping to take fish on the drop, you might want to make sure the

amount of solder applied allows the float to settle quite low. With practice you will find that it is possible to make a float that is loaded but needs no shot on the line at all, which will make it ideal for taking fish on the drop. It is also worth remembering that the more solder you add the more accurate they are. They will go further and the aim so precise that, the first time you cast with this new float, you will think that Phil Taylor has thrown it.

9 Now that you have decided on the amount of solder take a piece of kitchen towel and dry it out thoroughly. When the float is completely dry; mix up another small batch of araldite and apply it to the area where the solder is. Just spread it around as if you are buttering your toast. If you've done this right it should look horrible, but don't worry it will work out fine.

10 All you need is a naked flame; a candle is probably best. What you have to do is hold the part of the float you have just daubed with the glue a couple of inches above the flame and rotate it with your fingers. The araldite will quickly go runny and will sink into the twist of the solder thus making a smooth joint between it and the float body. Once you have it looking as smooth as glass, take it away from the flame immediately because it will spoil just as quickly. This process should take only a few seconds, be careful with the candle and blow it out as soon as you are done.

11 The float should now be propped up so that the glue isn't touching any other surfaces and left to dry. It is probably best to leave it overnight and the following day it can be painted in the colours of your desire.

Obviously now you've only got one new float and the whole thing seemed a bit tedious, but next time you can set up a production line and make a big batch all with different loadings, and I'm sure you will find this much more rewarding.

Quick Tip

Go to your local model shop and buy some proper enamel paint. Using the harvest cream emulsion you had left over from painting your parlour just won't do. I know it means parting with some cash but just think of how much money you will be saving by not buying a new float every week.

Making a loaded float

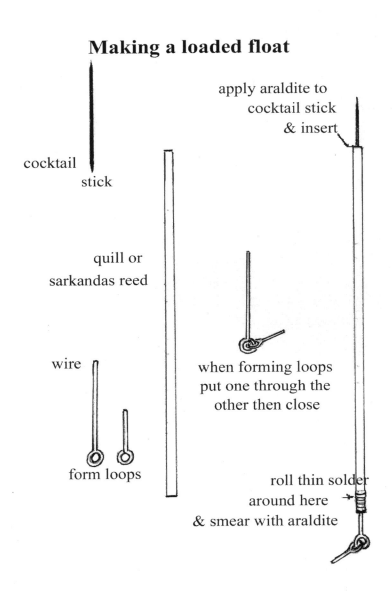

cocktail stick

apply araldite to cocktail stick & insert

quill or sarkandas reed

wire

when forming loops put one through the other then close

form loops

roll thin solder around here & smear with araldite

Tip 4:   Proper tackle

Fishing is sometimes all down to confidence and one way to make sure you aren't lacking in that department is to surround yourself with good quality tackle. It doesn't need to be top of the range, or be the latest craze to hit the market, but it has to be proper.

I have met all sorts of anglers, those with the newest and best of everything and, those other sort of anglers, the ones that will make do with odds and ends and the inheritance they got from their late uncle Bert's shed.

If you are like me, you would expect that out of the two anglers described the former would catch more fish. He might not be the best angler of course and this is often the case, but the seed is set in your mind. So if you fail to equip yourself with serviceable tackle it will sap your own confidence without you even knowing it. Here are three examples of anglers making do, when they should have invested in some proper tackle.

Johnny was a nice guy, but he had a thing about rod rests. He wouldn't buy one, he much preferred to find a stick with a "v" in the end and use that. Whenever you were fishing with him he'd always be scouring the bushes, rummaging in hedges and climbing trees to see if he could find one that was a better shape or longer than the one he'd got.

On one occasion when sport was slow I asked him about his wooden rod rest. All he would say was, why waste money on a bit of metal when the wooden ones are free. I tried listing the attributes of a proper rod rest, like length, and the ability to be pushed into hard ground, but it made no difference, he's still using a hazel nut twig and ever more shall do so.

Kevin was another fisherman who had a blind spot when it came to tackle. His nemesis was the accessory box, the one where you keep your floats, hooks, plummets and all the other paraphernalia that makes angling such an absorbing hobby.

He took up fishing at the relatively late age of nineteen and to help him get some kit together, the landlord of his local pub offered him an empty cigar display box for his nick-nacks as he called them. This was one of those boxes that had a perspex lid and was divided up into compartments to display cigars of various shapes and sizes.

Apparently, the bottom had dropped out of the cigar market, so the landlord was as pleased to dump it on Kevin, as Kevin was to receive it. I suppose it could've been the dog's bollocks, but in reality it would've been better described as like having tits on a bull. The compartments weren't big enough to take his floats, so he spent a whole weekend modifying it, but even then it still wasn't right. It was too big to lie flat in his tackle box, so it had to go in on its edge and that, I can tell you, is not the best thing to do with an accessory box.

A loud scream of anguish would often shatter the peace for miles around and bring forth unwelcome stares from other anglers who would be wondering what the heck was to do.

I mentioned the fact that his cigar accessory box wouldn't lie flat in the bottom of his tackle box. Well, the lid was apt to come open especially if the silly little hook and eye that held it shut had come adrift, and this is what happened on more than one occasion. We would turn up at a fishery, quietly pick our pegs and everything would be peaceful. Anglers would be speaking in whispers, the birds would be singing and every now and then there would be a splash as some joyful fish surfaced in this idyllic paradise.

A loud, "Oh no, I don't bastard well believe it!" sort of ruins the ambience.

Oh dear, the contents of Kevin's accessory box have dumped themselves into the bottom of his tackle box again, what a shame. Come on Kevin, get it together and get some proper kit.

The last of my examples regarding the need for proper kit comes from one of our sister sports of trout fishing. You know that one where you have to stand up all day thrashing the rod in the air like a mad conductor, and if you are lucky, you get to go home with a couple of fish that pound for pound have cost as much as a new rod.

Well one of our brethren, Bob, had just taken up the sport and talked me into accompanying him to an exclusive water that he'd blagged his way into fishing. We were greeted with a car park full of Range Roverish type vehicles and a couple of acres of water that was surrounded by a landscape that looked more like a garden. Trimmed bushes and closely cut grass was the order of the day here. It could have been the work of Capability Brown (now there's a funny first name) but he'd been dead a bit by then. It was a strange place for a fishery and I felt quite out of place. One look at the anglers, with their Barbour waistcoats, waxed jackets and creased trousers was enough to make me realise this branch of the sport wasn't for me.

Anyway, we set up, tied on a couple of flies out of Bob's fantastic collection of five and were soon swishing our rods with the rest of them. Although we were working hard, sport was at least by coarse fishing standards, extremely slow. Nothing was happening except the onset of a bad case of arm ache. Even the manikins were struggling, and if they couldn't catch then I reckoned neither would we.

I suppose we'd been at it for about an hour, in which time we'd been totally ignored by the other fishermen, so perhaps they could tell that we were impostors. Anyway, I don't know what happened but it seemed as if a trout suffering from suicidal tendencies (remember these barbarians don't put their fish back, they eat them) threw itself onto Bob's hook. It looked like a good one too as the rod was nearly bent double, then I realised that these flimsy rods would bend double if you tackled anything bigger than a stickleback with one of them. But regardless of that we were suddenly the centre of attention, and the angler next to us looked totally amazed. He put down his rod and sauntered over with his landing net to help Bob land it.

"Well done old chap, looks like you've bagged yourself a lovely rainbow," said the well-dressed angler with the handle bar moustache. "What did you take him on?" he went on to enquire.

"A pearly pennel," Bob replies and saw by the moustache's smile that he had gained his respect. I was impressed too, until I remembered he only had five flies so recalling their names shouldn't have been that difficult even for Bob.

Anyway, Bob won the battle with the fish that soon found itself enfolded in the net of the moustached one, who had been pleased to oblige. I suppose this was when things took a turn for the worse, and I also ought to mention that this incident actually happened in the seventies, a time when men wore flared trousers, had permed hair and you could still get pop in glass bottles.

Finally all the splashing was over and the fish was laid out on the manicured grass to be admired.

"Lovely fish," said him of the whiskers, and I agreed. The fish gasped and I could hardly look because I knew what was going to happen next, he was going to be dispatched into the next world, but because Bob was new at this game, he hadn't got a proper priest with which to do the deed. I can still remember how far the man's handlebar moustache drooped as we watched Bob beat that lovely fish to death with an empty coke bottle.

The old saying, "I wish the earth could have swallowed me up," had never seemed so apt.

So don't make do and mend, this is your chosen sport, it's what you do to relax, so make sure you have the right kit for the job.

Tip 5: The disgorger

A disgorger is probably the cheapest piece of fishing equipment you will ever buy, but one of the most important.

I like to think, and do actually believe, that the majority of anglers care deeply for the welfare of the fish we catch. It is important that when we catch a fish it is treated with respect and returned to the water as quickly as possible.

If a fish is hooked deeper than normal one of the easiest ways to remove a hook, especially on smaller fish, is to use a disgorger. In fact, using a disgorger is often easier than locating it. More often than not, you'll find yourself with one hand ferreting about in your box looking for it, while you have a frantic fish flapping about in the other. You can't see the wood for the trees and the more frustrated you get, the harder it is to find.

The answer is easy, put it on a piece of cord and wear it around your neck. Put it on when you tackle up and it will save you and more importantly the fish, a whole lot of unnecessary stress.

Tip 6: Nets

If there is one item of tackle that is often treated badly, it's the net. I guess part of the problem is that they smell so bad after a session that they are dumped down the shed out of the way before the wife can find the phone number for the solicitors.

The keepnet

I know they are not allowed in most fisheries now unless you are fishing a match, which in some ways is a bit of a shame. I used to enjoy seeing my day's work at the end of a session and, if the mesh was right and the net had been pegged out properly, I'm sure that the fish came to no harm. I also have this sneaking feeling, that when I put a fish straight back into the water, it's going to tell all its mates about the nasty angler on the bank and they'll go elsewhere and find some nice natural food to eat.

Anyway, I'm sure that those who make up the rules have the welfare of the fish upper most in their minds, so I'm happy to go along with the no keepnet rule, after all the fish must come first.

If you are only using your keepnet for matches it is twice as important to look after it. When you get back after a match don't just stick it in the shed, peg it out on the lawn and wash it down with the hose pipe and, while you're at it, rinse out the bag you keep it in. The net will last longer and will be less likely to fall prey to mice and other rodents that could give it a little chewing. They don't want to eat it of course they just can't stop nibbling and a fishy tasting net makes a nice change from boring old cardboard.

I bet most of you have come across the following scenario; I know I have on more than one occasion. You are following the weigh-in down the towpath or the riverbank after a match, when you come to some smug bastard who's been bagging up all day. He stands there grinning like a griffin, well why not he's confident he's done the business. He's got one hand on his net and a smile on his face like a cat that'd just eaten your favourite goldfish.

"What's winning so far?" he asks nonchalantly because he knows he's got it beat. Then he drags his net from the water while calculating how much pools money he's won and which shelf he's going to put the trophy on.

"Bloody hell, I don't believe it!" he cries out in anguish as he sees that his keepnet is empty. The anglers who are watching the weigh-in make a show of false sympathy.

"Oh dear Mike, that's a shame I think you've got a hole in your net," says one of the anglers, but their faces are smiling and telling the truth which is aptly summed up by an angler at the back.

"It couldn't have happened to a nicer bloke," he says and they all titter. So always wash your net and, before a match, always give it a quick check for holes.

Landing net

A hole in a landing net isn't as bad as a hole in the keep net that's for sure, but it can cause trouble, so while you are hosing down your keepnet and pegging it out to dry, do the same with your landing net.

I have always been a great believer in fine presentation and thus have always used light tackle. This means that I get more bites but at a cost of not being able to bully my fish in. I have to take my time and play them for a little longer than those using big tackle. One day I was fishing one of those small pools that seem to be springing up everywhere. A couple of acres in size, it was surrounded by about thirty anglers, everybody could see everybody, hear what everybody else was saying and if I was using a pole I could've almost touched tips with the angler opposite. Anyway, I made a real twit of myself that morning and haven't been back to the venue since.

All was going well; I'd had a few small fish and seemed to be doing much better than everybody else. It was slightly embarrassing because every time I caught a fish I could hear mutterings from some of the other anglers like, "he's got another one," and "jammy bastard."

Then it all came undone; I struck into a bigger fish, a carp of about four pounds. Not a monster, but on my light tackle it would be a handful. I let it have a couple of good runs before putting a bit more pressure on in an effort to get it to the net quickly. Every angler around that pool was watching me so I didn't want to make a meal of it. Finally, it was within reaching distance of the net, the fish had stopped struggling briefly and just like a professional I slid the net under it with the satisfaction only anglers can appreciate.

But just as quickly as the fish went in, it came out again through a hole I hadn't noticed in the bottom. It also felt stronger than ever and made a dash for the middle of the pool and left me looking like a right wally. My line didn't go straight to the fish, it went via my landing net through the hole in the bottom. Was I in a pickle, I could hear the other anglers having a bit of a giggle.

"What's the idiot up to now?" and "I don't know, he's a bloody twerp," were two that I can distinctly remember. So, wash your nets after every session; then put them in a safe place away from mice, squirrels and other beasts with serious teeth. But most important of all, check them thoroughly for holes before you start fishing.

Quick tip

If you've been waiting a long time for a bite, give the handle of your reel a couple of quick turns. This often induces a nearby fish, who perhaps isn't that hungry, to take the bait. It's a bit like pulling a ball of wool for a cat. I once fished a match where this was the only way I could get a bite and at the end of the competition I'd almost tripled the weight of the next angler.

Tip 7: Choosing a rod

Fishing rods have, by and large, caused me very little in the way of problems. I have always been satisfied, regardless of the materials from which they were made. Having said that; I have actually purchased very few rods and poles. I guess it's because I have always been a follower when it comes to new technology. It's rare in any field of life that the perfect article comes out with the first edition.

Washing powder is a prime example; the adverts on the telly say it all. "Try 'Wonder Wash,' and get your whites, whiter than white, new improved formula." Computer software is another product that is always evolving. A new version of software is always on the way or patches are made available to fix the flaws.

And so it has been with fishing rods, each time the technology changed, I didn't rush out and buy the first one, I waited. By the way, if we go back to the seventies again, there was an even bigger example of what I am talking about.

Somebody somewhere invented the digital watch. It seems daft now, but people actually went and drooled over the first one that was displayed in our local jeweller's window. They had to drool because none of them could afford to pay over £300 for a watch; it would've taken the average worker six weeks to earn that amount of cash. Anyway, expecting people to pay silly money for a watch wasn't going to last long and it didn't, by the end of the decade garages were handing them out for free when you bought a gallon of petrol. Now everybody, except that is for a few treckies, have returned to the old dial face, funny old world ain't it.

Back to the rods and the first one I had the pleasure of owning. It was a two-piece cane, my dad bought it for me and I can remember catching a few fish with it. Sometimes, I caught even more than him despite his being quite a bit longer. My father's rod came in three pieces and the tip section was very special because it was made from split cane.

Originally his rod was just a three-piece cane sort, cheap and run of the mill. But one day, when my elder brother Edgar and I went with him on a trip down the river, we had a disaster. Well my dad's rod did, he put it down on the grass to unhook a fish and my brother trampled on the thin end, smashing it to smithereens.

The air was blue for the rest of the day, but my dad took it to somebody who built rods and he made him a tip section from split cane. I can still remember the red and green whippings; it was a thing of real beauty. As soon as I could afford it I purchased a split cane rod of my own and it gave me good service. However, I eventually went the way of the rest and invested in a model made from fibre-glass, which had been all the rage for a couple of years.

I suppose I'd just about got my money's worth out of that technology when carbon-fibre arrived with a bang and a hefty price tag. It was a bit like the watch story; the prices of the first ones on the market seemed to be extortionate. So I didn't bother getting caught up with the panic, I took my time and waited, I knew they wouldn't be giving them away with petrol, but the quality would increase and the prices would drop to a level that I was comfortable paying.

In the end I picked a rod that was reasonably priced and had an action that suited my style. By that I mean I'm a bit twitchy when it comes to striking and apt to go off like a mousetrap and this can lead to breakages. As already discussed, line with some stretch helps but a rod that has some forgiveness in the tip is also good.

Quick tip

Go steady with the polish. I say this to save you the embarrassment I heaped onto myself.

Pole fishing had become all the rage and I joined in with the rest of them and was soon practising the art of unshipping and joining pole sections together. This was in the days before the paint roller type rests had been invented, and to bring a fish in from the far side of the canal the only way was to take each section of pole off, one at a time.

I am sure that anglers today would laugh till they burst if they could see the clumsy pioneers of this method in action. During the unshipping process, sections of pole would be dropped into the water or the angler would lift the pole too early and struggle to reach a fish that was swinging freely above his head like a death defying trapeze artist.

Part of the problem was the joints of the pole didn't part easily, so I put my thinking cap on and came up with the idea of polishing the joints. It worked great and I should have left it there, but one day, after a session with my rod, I had a job to part the first two sections so, when I got home, the polish came out again. Anyway, the following week saw me sitting at the side of a gravel pit in Derbyshire. I had a long featureless bank and a huge expanse of water in front of me and was flanked by my mates from the angling club. The apprehension was growing as we all waited patiently for the whistle and the shout of "all in."

My mind was going over the plan I'd hatched the night before. Ignore the pole, go for distance with the waggler, loose feed maggots over a bed of hemp and alternate between caster and maggot on the hook until I find out which gives the best results.

Why is it that the match secretary's watch is always slow? The match was supposed to start at eight o'clock but it was almost five past when the signal for the start came, and by then my nerves were tighter than Eric Clapton's guitar strings.

Anyway, I went for the big one, beach caster style and watched as the top two sections of my rod left me and took off into the distance like a javelin that had been thrown by Fatima Whitbread.

So go steady on the polish, what might be good for poles is not so good for rods.

Tip 8:   Overloading yourself

Fishing is a sport that is evolving but in a crazy sort of way. Sometimes, I have to convince myself that I'm not watching an episode of the world's strongest man. Gone are the days when all anglers were burdened under a common load. Tackle box over one shoulder and rod bag over the other. One hand held a net bag and the other was free to help you over styles, and open gates etc.

There are a still few anglers who approach the water in this style, but they are a dying breed. Most now seem to need at least two rod bags, a tackle box and a hold-all that would see a family of four through a week's self-catering in Lanzarote. They also have a giant net bag which they carry everywhere, even to venues where nets are banned. But worst of all is the man mountain that has brought enough stuff with him to be able to service a small fleet of cars. So much stuff does this man need to catch a few fish that he not only adorns himself with rod bags and tackle boxes, he pushes before him a wheel barrow type contraption that is stacked so high, he can't see where he's going.

He arrives at the water after everybody else because he's had to load all of this tackle into his car. It takes him longer to get to his peg and is even restricted by lack of access to some because of his load. It also takes him twice as long as everybody else to set up because he's got so many rods. Yes he's paid for them, so he's going to make damn well sure he uses them. When he starts fishing he's got that much tackle that he's simply spoiled for choice. On top of that, he is now completely knackered. If he'd walked that far with all that tackle in Nepal he'd have been able to hire himself half a dozen Sherpas, but he's done it on his own, so instead of enjoying his fishing he's looking forward to going home for a nice long sleep. He probably would do too; it's only the thought of packing all that kit away that is keeping him on the bank.

So the next time you go fishing, take a sideways glance at your reflection in the lake and if you recognise this man and he looks like the one already described. Do yourself a favour, get rid of the clutter, get back to basics and take with you only the kit you need for that session, it's got to make sense.

Tip 9: Bait waiter

A bait waiter was one of the best fishing purchases I ever made. It was cheap, held four boxes and there was even enough space in the middle for a cup of tea. The difference it made to my comfort when fishing was immense. In fact, I'd put it on a par with getting a remote control for the telly. Remember life without one of those little beauties, when you had to get up and walk over to the telly just to change the channel.

Not only does a bait waiter stop you having to keep bending down every time you want some bait for your hook, or to loose feed, it also frees up space at the side of you. It might not be very often but it can also alert you to the fact that your bait is escaping. Think about those misty drizzly days, the ones that your wife complains make her hair go frizzy. One of those days when the fish aren't playing ball and you are so miserable, you can't be bothered to put your brolly up. It isn't proper rain you say to yourself, just a bit of drizzle, a few spots of water never hurt anybody.

The trouble is that twenty minutes later, when you bend down to get a pinkie for your hook, you find that 90% of your bait has gone. There is nothing like a bit of damp on the inside of a bait box to awaken the climber in maggots and pinkies.

Excuse me if I digress a bit here, but please consider the following anecdote before you put anything sticky on your maggots. Think first because they'll be out of your bait box faster than workers leaving a factory when the hooter blows on a Friday afternoon.

Putting a powder that was supposed to make you a nice bedtime drink onto your bait to make it sticky, was one of those fashions that came into the world of fishing during the seventies. The crux of the idea was that if you sprinkled a spoonful of the powder onto your maggots, it made them stick together and therefore easier to pick up a few at a time. They could be rolled into a ball and you could then throw this concentrated ball into a precise target area. In other words it would keep your loose feed together, rather than scattering it and your fish all over the place. Well, I gave it a go; after all I was always on the lookout for something to give me the edge over my fellow competitors.

I tried out my new secret weapon at a match on the river Trent in Nottinghamshire. I set up full of confidence because the conditions were perfect, I had drawn a good peg, and my plan I hoped, was going to be a masterstroke. On the night before the match I had been crafty, as soon as my wife had made our bedtime drinks, I took the jar back out of the cupboard and slipped it into my box. What she didn't know about couldn't hurt her, as long as I remembered to put it back in its rightful place after the fishing match, all would be well with the world.

Anyway, I was all set up with three pints of maggots and a pint of hemp on my bait waiter. I got the jar and sprinkled it on two of them. I left the lid on the third box just in case something silly happened and my waiter got knocked over or something.

The whistle went and I rolled a ball of maggots in my hand and plopped them into the river about a rod length out and followed this with a small handful of hemp.

I was impressed with the accuracy I attained with the ball of maggots and was sure it was going to be a winner. I repeated the process a few times but then I became concerned about my fingers, they were getting a bit uncomfortable and making my rod sticky. In fact, everything was getting sticky including my reel handle and the bale arm. To make matters even worse I noticed the maggots were climbing up the side of my bait box and escaping like rats from a sinking ship. I put the lid on one box to save as many as possible and tried to carry on fishing but it was hard work and ruined my concentration. Every time I put my hand into my box for some maggots I had to swish it around the side to knock some off in an effort to stop them getting away.

It was a five hour match, but in less than two and despite all my efforts to stop them absconding, I had used two pints of bait. Well, let me put that another way I'd used about a quarter of a pint, the rest had taken their chance and fled, I'm sure I could hear them laughing at me as they made their bid for freedom.

So get yourself a bait waiter, but think twice before you put anything sticky on your maggots.

Tip 10: A good brolly

An umbrella is one of the most important items a fisherman can buy, so make sure you get a good one. I've seen brollys advertised that are shower proof only, now I ask you, is there anything more useless in this life than an umbrella that doesn't stop proper rain?

Not only should a brolly be waterproof but it should also be sturdy even when a gale is blowing. Sitting in the calm under the shelter of a good brolly when the world is raging around you is a pleasure; it makes you feel safe and sort of cosy.

Beside wind and rain, my brolly has also shielded me from some man made dangers. The first of these was when I was fishing a lake near to where I live. The lake is situated along the edge of a nine-hole golf course and some of the pegs are very close to the holes. In golfing terms I would reckon it would be no more than a good eight iron. Anyway, I was advised by the match secretary that, because I'd drawn a peg near one of these holes, I should put my umbrella up straight away to shield me from any wayward golf shots.

I laughed when he said it and ignored his advice but, after the "all in," I found I couldn't concentrate properly because I was waiting for one of those hard white balls to hit me on the back of the head. I don't know about you, but I've always had a vision of passing away quietly in a warm bed, not being found dead with a split cranium on peg twelve.

So I put my brolly up and I don't know if it was just good fortune or what, but two golf balls hit it during the course of that match and I reckon either one of them could have done for me.

The second incident was during one of those mid-week sessions that you have after work in the summer. My job had been a bastard all day and I just wanted to get away, so I went to a small pond not far from home. It's a lovely little pool in a small valley, but because it's a two-field walk from the road it isn't very popular with other anglers. I don't know what it is with some fishing folk, you'd think they were lame. A lot of them will only fish where they can park their vehicles behind their tackle boxes. In fact, I'm pretty sure that some of them would fish through their car windows if they could get away with it.

Sorry, I'll get back to the point in hand. I set myself up in a lovely little peg that was flanked by Canadian pondweed on both sides and another clump in front of me about two rod lengths out. There was a small wood behind, which was sheltering me nicely from a stiff breeze. I was using maggots for bait; these were leftovers from the weekend. All was going well and I was catching regularly, only small roach and perch but nice fish all the same. The serenity however was soon shattered when a loud bang came from behind me, it was so close and sudden that it made me jump.

"What the bloody hell," I shouted to myself and then I realised that somebody had fired a shotgun on the other side of the wood. I sat down and carried on fishing half expecting it to go off again. A short while later it did and a split second afterwards another strange thing happened. A shower of something hit the water in front of me; it was as if a ghost angler had just decided to feed my swim with a catapult full of hemp.

I didn't understand what was going on. I hadn't got any hemp, so perhaps I was finally going mad and entering a parallel world. While I was scratching my head and still pondering the mystery of the hemp, the gun when off again. And, like before it was followed by the strange feeding of my swim. Bingo, I worked it out that the bang of the gun and the feeding of the swim were linked, and I deduced even faster that if this was the case then the stuff that was feeding my swim was shotgun pellets.

So what do you do, run through the woods, seek out the deadly assassin and give him a piece of your mind. Well I tell you what I did; I recalled the golf balls on peg twelve and went straight for my trusty umbrella.

Yes I can hear you laughing; a brolly won't stop shotgun pellets. I know that and I'd have to agree, but these pellets weren't hitting the water horizontally they were coming down like a shower of rain and somehow it just made me feel safer.

There was only one more bang that evening and I think one or two pellets might have bounced off my shelter. The hit man disappeared but I was left with a feeling of apprehension that would have been much worse it if wasn't for that safe feeling you get with a good umbrella.

Tips Section 3: Matches

I know some anglers have never fished a match in their lives and there are just as many who have no intention of ever doing so, but if you are one of them please don't skip this section. Most of the tips included here lend themselves to anglers who fish for pleasure just as much as for those who seek fame and glory.

Tip 1: Never leave your peg

Yes I know this is one of those rules that is ignored by lots of match anglers but that doesn't mean you have to do it. I can honestly say that during all the years that I've fished in competitions, I never left my peg; that is except for a call of nature. Don't get the idea that I'm some sort of goody-goody because a saint I ain't. I just reckon that if a competition is five hours long then I need to fish for the whole five hours, there will be plenty of time to go walk about when it's all over.

I have sometimes wondered how this rule came about. It could have been to save damage to the fish, because I know that some anglers are apt to leave their bait in the water when they leave their pegs. There again it might have been to stop cheating, if you are catching nothing and the angler two pegs away is bagging up you might want to go and stand behind him for a bit and see what he's doing and what bait he's using, then go and copy him.

Whatever the reason, I think the rule is a good one, especially if it stops people from cheating. There will be more on that subject in a later chapter, but for now let's understand why it is better not to leave your peg during a match.

The main reason I have slavishly followed the rule, is because you never know what is going to happen while you are away. The most obvious thing is that you can miss a fish. It's Sod's law that you can sometimes go without a bite for hours; you sit there wondering why you don't take up origami to put some excitement back into your life; then all of a sudden there is a twitch, your float is gone and you strike much too late.

Of course the good anglers among us are ready for this, but the weaker ones always miss out. Sometimes it's as if the fish are watching what you are doing. You take your eye off the float for a second to pick up your flask and when you look back your float is just coming back up. Or you stand up to take a leak, and for hygiene's sake you move at least a couple of feet from your peg before doing the deed. But even as you are doing it, you are looking over your shoulder waiting for it to happen. You may not have had so much as a nibble for the last half hour, but your float still goes under as if by magic. Your hands are full and you've missed another bite and what's even more infuriating is that you know it could've been the winner.

So, if the fish are going to watch you and take advantage of you when you are pouring some coffee or taking a pee, just think what they'd get up to if you left your peg.

There are few matches where anglers catch fish from beginning to end. The usual pattern is for the fishing to start off slow while more fish are attracted; sport will then improve to a peak and then slowly die away. During this natural cycle there can be periods of rapid action and equally some periods when nothing happens at all. For me this can be the most interesting time in a match, trying to catch one more fish when everybody else has lost the will to live has worked for me on a number of occasions. In fact, I have lost count of the times when a single fish has been the difference between me coming in the frame and failing altogether.

If it's a gudgeon bashing match down the canal, a bonus perch can make all the difference. Likewise if you are fishing a match on a river, a good chub can see you going home with a pocket full of lolly. Be it a perch or a chub, it's one bite, and that one might just happen while you are away from your peg.

Now, the tale I'm about to tell you proves the point about not leaving your peg. Another angler told me this story a couple of days after he'd witnessed the action, and he swore every word was true.

The incident took place during a club match on the river Trent when my friend Ben, was pegged between two fishermen who had great disregard for each other, in other words they hated each other's guts.

It was one of those matches where nothing much was happening, the fish weren't biting and, to make matters worse, a flotilla of dinghies came sailing around the bend. Things weren't going to get much better while these boats passed and that was going to take a while because they were not only sailing against the current, they were also fighting the wind which was blowing in the opposite direction. Those with nautical tendencies will know that this means they have to zig-zag across the river or tack, as it is known in sailing circles.

Anyway, misery guts angler number one decides he's fed up and goes walk about. While he's gone, one of the boats catches a good gust and scurries straight into his peg and dumps two sailors on top of his tackle. They of course are full of embarrassment and couldn't get back on their yacht quick enough. They put the angler's rod back on its rest, hopped back onto their boat and they're gone. All seemed well except the top foot of the rod that belongs to misery guts number one, is hanging down like a swing tip. My friend looks over to misery guts angler number two to see if he had seen the occurrence and he obliviously had because he smiled back smugly, and said, "serves the bloody bastard right."

They both waited patiently for the return of misery guts number one, it would be a treat to observe the look on his face when he saw what the sailors had done to his rod. The only trouble was, he didn't know that the dingy or its crew had been anywhere near his tackle, so when he came back and saw that the end of his rod had been broken, he snapped to the conclusion that it must have been the work of his arch enemy, misery guts angler number two. Without further thought he went round to his peg and smacked him in the gob. The result of this was fists flying everywhere and half a dozen other anglers having to put their rods down to break up the fight. Both anglers were suspended from the club until further notice.

So don't leave your peg, unless you want to lose the winning fish, be involved in a fight or have your rod broken by a clumsy sailor.

Tip 2: Provide your own bait

I know it's often a bit of trouble to get your own bait, especially in this busy age when sometimes it's a job to find even enough time to breathe. But if you are serious about match fishing it makes sense to provide your own bait.

During my early match fishing career, I would get my bait as cheaply as possible from whatever source was available. It took me a while to realise it, but this cheap and convenient bait wasn't the best. If I was fishing a match where bloodworm and joker was allowed, I knew that I'd have to obtain some of this expensive bait if I was to have any chance of winning. Luckily there was always somebody who was willing to provide some for me and other anglers.

The morning of the match would arrive and he who said he was getting the bait would deal out the newspaper packages containing the bloodworm and jokers like portions of fish and chips. There wasn't time to inspect the contents, but I was always shocked to find that it was mostly peat. While fishing I would have to dig about looking for a suitable specimen to put on the hook and I would have to be very mean when feeding the joker or it would be gone in the first hour.

It took me a while to cotton on, but guess who always did well in these matches? Yes, the fellow that supplied the bait. I must have been a bit thick in those days and hadn't put two and two together, but I believe now that when he purchased the bait, he sorted out a nice batch for himself and repackaged the remaining rubbish for the rest of us.

The sad and only thing any of us did was have a good old moan that the bait wasn't very good. The supplier would look at us with a disgruntled face and tell us how hard it was to find, and if we didn't like it we were welcome to get our own, which with hindsight is exactly what we should have done.

I had another strange issue with bait that I'm still not sure about and it follows a similar pattern. The bait this time was casters, which were ordered from a fellow angler who always reared his own.

We would have to order the bait a week in advance and he would turn up with it on the day of the match. Well, at one of these matches he was late arriving and me and a couple of other anglers who had ordered bait from him were beginning to get worried.

Anyway, we had all drawn our pegs and were milling around muttering indecently about our bait supplier when he turned up in a right fluster. He quickly made his draw while we all gathered around the boot of his car each with a bait box in hand. It was customary for him to open a bag of casters and pour some into each angler's bait box.

The pattern today was just the same, but as the bait was poured into the boxes something was amiss because in the middle of my pile of casters was a big, crisp, pickled onion.

As I looked in amazement, one of my mates also discovered an extra morsel of the same description.

"What the bloody hell is that?" he demanded, while pointing at the offending lump.

"Ha, just having a joke," said the bait-pickler, "chuck them away and I'll get you some more." He then delved into his box and came out with another bag of casters, which we all gratefully received and went off to our pegs.

It could've been a joke of course, and perhaps it was, but it left me with an uneasy feeling. Not only could an unscrupulous person make money from supplying bait to other anglers, they could also ruin the winning chances of those that they'd supplied. In this case the bait supplier passed away a few weeks later and left me not knowing if it was a joke or not.

I have also heard about another person, through a non-angler, who knew nothing about the sport and he reckoned an acquaintance of his bragged about how he cheated at fishing. Apparently, he also supplied bait to other anglers and liked to swill the casters he was providing around in a tiny amount of paraffin. Not enough to make them smell, but strong enough for the taste to put the fish off.

No, I don't believe a fellow angler would do that I hear you cry in anguish. Well I'm glad to say that most anglers wouldn't, but when money and prestige are involved I'm afraid I can believe it. There will be more on cheats a little later, but for me the message is clear, supply your own bait and at least you'll know where it has come from.

Tip 3: Remove the slime

If there is one thing that makes my stomach turn, it's watching somebody fish with a great load of fish slime dangling between their bottom shot and their hook. Two species of fish are the main culprits, the bream and the tench. The slime gets onto the line when it comes into contact with the flank of the fish as it is being played before bringing it to the net.

I know it's a bind to get rid of and all you want to do is cast in again as fast as possible to bag a similar specimen, but please clean your line first. Get your finger and thumb by your hook, where the slime usually starts, and pull it up toward your bottom shot. That should remove most of it, but do pay attention to the hook, it must be spotless. The only thing that should ever be on a hook is nice fresh clean bait that you have supplied yourself. Sorry, you already know all that.

"Why should it matter if there's a bit of slime on my line?" I hear you ask. "It is fish slime, so it's quite natural to the fish, in actual fact it belongs to them."

I know it does, and they are usually wearing it, not seeing it in great lines along the bottom of the lake. I know they aren't very bright but they do have instinct, so when they see the slime that they know one of their friends should be wearing, and it's attached to a bunch of maggots, they are apt to give it a wide berth.

Trust me, you will get very few bites until you clean your line, so do it every time you catch a tench or a bream, it works for me.

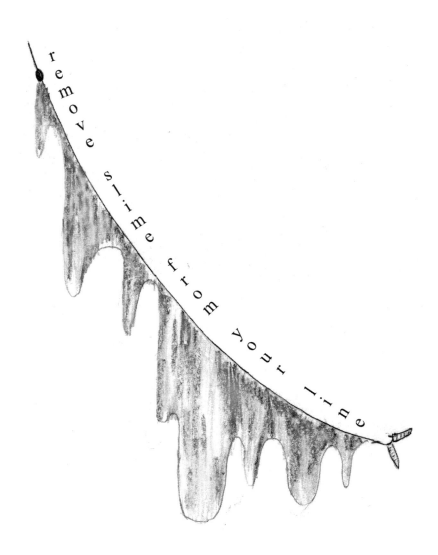

remove slime from your line

Tip 4: Target weight

I can't remember where this tip originally came from, but I think I must have read it somewhere. It was one of those concepts that didn't sink in straight away; it just sort of nagged away at me until the proverbial penny actually dropped.

I had always approached competitive fishing in the same way. My aim would be to go to the water and catch as many fish as I could, hopefully bigger and more than anybody else. This was a simple plan, if indeed you could call it a plan, and needless to say it was seldom very successful. Then one day, after reading an article about target weights it all started to get a bit clearer, like watching a bus coming out of the fog.

From that point onwards my thoughts about the next match took a new direction. I would not just take my favourite bait and hope for the best, I would think it all through logically. During this process my mind returned to the tip that I had read about. The starting point was now obvious, if I wanted to win or do well in the forthcoming match I needed to answer just one question. What weight would I have to put on the scales to win it? Once that was known I could set my stall out accordingly and put together a winning plan.

"Yeah, but how do you know what's going to win a match?" I hear you ask. "It could be anything, depends on the time of the year and all that."

Okay, some of that is true, but as likely as not, you know the venue that you are going to fish, and if you are honest with yourself, you know roughly what the winning weight is likely to be. When I fished a series of matches on my local canal I knew that anybody who managed to catch over three pounds would more than likely be in the frame and on most occasions they'd win it.

So I stopped going with a view to catching as much and as many big fish as possible, I went with a focused objective and that was to catch at least three pounds of fish. It was a bit like being in Africa with your best mate and being chased by a lion. You don't have to run faster than the lion just faster than your mate. In other words don't just aim to catch a lot, aim for the least that will bring you success.

I can still remember those canal matches vividly. I would start with a whip just over the near shelf with a rig that would put the bait down quickly. Very soon a procession of gudgeon would find their way to the keep net. These were small fish and weighed about 3 to the ounce, so my objective was to catch 144, which would make up my target of 3 pounds of fish. But I even went further than that; I calculated that because the bites would dwindle during the match I ought to be aiming for 64 fish in the first hour when the venue would be at its best.

During the following hour if I could get another 48 fish bringing my tally to 112, I would be well on my way to my target and still have 3 hours to fish. These last few hours of the match were always the hardest and there was a steady decline in bites during this time due to the reduced numbers of fish available and increased boat traffic.

I would, of course, have been forming a plan for the last three hours during the first two and this would often depend on what the far bank looked like. If there was cover over there in the form of weeds or some overhanging branches then I would feed the area a little before giving it a go. I would be hoping to pick up a few nice roach or even some more gudgeon.

I would also keep feeding my original killing zone but very lightly. I would come back to this periodically to give the far bank a rest and to pick up a few bonus gudgeon. I would also alter my rig for this by sliding my weight up the line. The reason for this was because the gudgeon were now few and far between there was no need to get the bait onto the bottom so quickly, but there was however, a real chance of picking up some small roach or perch on the drop.

Using this method, I managed when fishing most matches, to catch my 144 fish or at least a number that would roughly equal the same weight. The result was that, for two years in succession, I won the championship by quite a big margin and I'm sure it wouldn't have happened if I hadn't concentrated on catching my target weight.

I think it's worth a mention here that one of the anglers who fished this championship every year had the same idea in mind, but he came at it from a different angle, if you'll please pardon the expression.

He was a rod man through and through and had no time for fishing with poles. He also knew that without using the pole fishing method, he couldn't compete in the gudgeon bashing stakes. So every match he went on he tried the same tactics. He would fish the far side, with a lump of bread flake, with the hope of hooking one of the few carp that were present in the water. He tried this method relentlessly, knowing that if he caught just one good fish it would be all over.

I have to take my hat off to him because he stuck to his task but, as far as I know, he only hooked a carp on one occasion and that just happened to be when I was pegged next to him. I guess we were about halfway through the match and I was catching steadily when I heard the splash opposite him. I looked over and his rod was bent almost double as the fish ran along the far margin in my direction.

"Got one of the bastards, and I'll tell you what Georgie boy, it's going to take some stopping," he said to me loudly, with a smile as big as a pardoned prisoner. Anyway, he was right, the fish would take some stopping, but he wasn't the man to do it. His clutch screamed and, with a bow wave that would've done a speedboat proud, the fish went past me at about ninety miles an hour and then managed to shed the old chap's hook. I can't remember his exact words but the air was blue. He stamped his feet, threw his rod into the hedge behind him and stalked off down the towpath in a great huff.

You would have thought this near miss would've spurred him on, but it wasn't to be. He fished a few more matches after his escapade with the carp, but his heart wasn't in it and he finally packed up match fishing altogether. This was a shame because he had the right idea, but it just wasn't viable for that water.

I have used the canal to illustrate the need for a target weight, but it is exactly the same no matter where you are fishing. If you haven't been to the venue before check the angling press to see what's been winning, or if you can, talk to somebody who has fished it. Once you know the target weight and the species the water holds, you should be able to put together a plan that at least gives you a fighting chance of winning, and that's got to be better than to just chuck and hope.

Tip 5: Watch out for cheats

I said a couple of chapters ago that I'd return to the subject of cheats, so we may as well get the thorny subject out of the way. Wherever money or pride is involved there will always be those who think the road to success is via a short cut. These people are often cheating on their friends, but they can, apparently, still manage to sleep soundly every night.

Thankfully, out and out cheating isn't rife in angling matches but it does happen. I was once involved with a knock out competition where two clubs would field a small team of anglers that would compete against each other on a neutral venue. The prize money was good, but just as attractive was an all-expenses paid trip to Ireland for the two teams that reached the final.

When it came to our match I wasn't actually fishing, but I'd been asked to run the bank, which under the rules of the competition was allowed. For those of you who have not heard the term "running the bank," it refers to having a person walk up and down the bank communicating with each member of the team. The sort of information passed on was, how well they were catching and were any particular baits doing well. Each angler was also expected to keep tabs on the opposition each side of them, to see how well they were catching. If one of them was doing particularly well, the bank runner could linger behind them for a while and report back accordingly. Having taken part in running the bank for a team I can say that it wasn't something

I'd be in favour of doing again, it seemed a bit like spying and I wasn't happy with the concept.

Right, let's get back to the plot because it's about to thicken. I did my job for the four hours of the match, continually going up and down the bank and my observations told me that we were winning. Every member of our team was catching steadily and they all reckoned they were beating the opposition easily. This tallied with what I'd seen during my frequent walks up and down the towpath and I was starting to think about the trip overseas.

Never count your chickens is a good saying, because after the weigh in we discovered we'd lost the match by ten ounces. We went back to our headquarters, well the Red Lion actually, and held a post mortem. We all agreed that we should have won because we knew we had caught more fish than them. But how had they done it?

"Perhaps it had something to do with the shifty looking guy on the bike who brought the bloke fishing next to me a flask of coffee," said Harry.

"Yeah I didn't like the look of him either," said Norman, "he gave the bloke next to me a flask of coffee or something as well."

I could also confirm seeing the man on the bike giving out a flask and that must have been how they'd done it. The flasks weren't full of coffee or tea; they were full of gudgeon and were quickly tipped into the anglers' keep nets when nobody was watching. Shame on them, of course our theory couldn't be proved and, if we brought it up, it would've only seemed like a case of sour grapes. There was nothing we could do about it, so we just put it down to experience.

My other encounter with cheating was by somebody I knew pretty well. His name was Greg, and because he was a policeman's son I think he should've known better.

We were fishing a small friendly match around a reed and tree fringed pool in Cheshire and because I'd drawn a peg only a couple from Greg, I went to have a quick chat with him during that horrible delay that comes between setting up and the start whistle.

While we were chatting there was a small splash in the reeds at the edge of his peg. We both looked and saw the sad sight of a fish going through its death-throws. It was a nice bream of about three pounds and, judging by the look of the gash on its flank, it must have had an unfriendly encounter with a pike.

"Wouldn't mind that in my net, I'd be half-way to winning the match," Greg said.

"You can't weigh dead fish in," I replied.

"It ain't dead yet," he said, and with that last remark I returned to my peg and thought nothing about it until after the match had finished.

At the weigh in it was soon clear that not much had been caught. Most anglers only had a few bits to put on the scales so anybody with a bonus fish would be in with a chance.

Well guess who had a bonus fish, a sickly looking bream of about three pounds.

"Bloody hell Greg," I said, "I bet that took some netting?"

He just shot me a filthy look that said, prove it or shut up. Well what could I do, I had no proof and to accuse him of cheating there and then in front of all those anglers would not be very pleasant. I had to make a split second decision and I decided to say nothing. One reason was because the fish was lying with its good side up; I couldn't very well grab it and turn it over without causing a commotion.

Anyway, as Greg emptied the fish back into the water I plainly saw the tell-tale slash made by the pike. There was no doubt in my mind that Greg had cheated but now the evidence was gone and for me to accuse him of foul play would have sounded a bit silly.

He pocketed the pools money and offered to take me for a drink, which I accepted. Greg didn't win very often and I suppose the temptation that was put in front of him was too great and in a minute of madness he succumbed and slipped a net under that sad bream. We still remained friends, but our relationship changed and I would never trust that man again. As it happens it didn't matter much because he moved to Canada about six months later.

So keep your eyes peeled for cheats. You can get a hell of a lot of gudgeon in an empty rod tube.

Tip 6: Feed with caution

This tip mainly concerns match fishing on canals but does lend itself to being useful elsewhere.

A lot of the matches I fish take place on canals. These long stretches of uniform water present a level playing field for all the competitors. A few pegs might be slightly deeper, or have a nice bit of cover on the far bank, but in reality they provide a venue where the skill of the angler comes to the fore.

They do of course have one drawback and that is the boats. I don't want to dwell here on the boats themselves or the holidaymakers who are apt to ground their forty footer right on the far bank where you happen to be catching. Yes, I could moan about boats all day if you get me started. What really gets my dander up is when a match has been arranged to start at 6 o'clock on a summer's morning in the hope of getting at least a couple of hours good fishing in before they start trawling the water, but before you've even finished the draw, Captain Pugwash comes chugging past at full throttle.

But that's enough of that; I don't want to talk about the boats, what I'm interested in is the side effect that comes with them, like the opening and closing of the locks. If you've fished canals you'll know what I mean, one minute the water is nice and calm and then all of a sudden it's running like a mountain stream.

Somebody has opened a lock or sluice gate to let the water out of one section or, pounds as they are known, into another. The rate of increased flow you suffer is governed by your distance from the lock and the difference in height between the two pounds. The closer you are and the higher the drop in level, the bigger will be the pull on the water. It's a bit like pulling the plug out of your bath. The closer the water gets to the plughole the quicker it goes down.

So now that you are aware of what is going on and I apologise to those of you who knew it already, we can get down to the point. If you are feeding your swim nicely, little and often and building up a good head of fish, the last thing you want to do is lose them. This is exactly what can happen if you feed just at the moment when a lock is being opened. Whoosh the water moves and so does your feed. But worse than that, half of the fish you had in your swim have gone off chasing it down stream. By the time the water comes to a halt again they could be several pegs away.

This is a disaster and ranks with scoring a goal in your own net when playing football. It's no good calling foul and saying it wasn't your fault because you didn't know when the lock was going to open, it was just bad luck. Well actually it wasn't just bad luck, there are a couple of things that will help you avoid this disaster.

The first thing is to understand the water and have at least some idea of how far away the nearest locks are both upstream and down. Armed with this information you can improve your situation by at least 50%, because you will be able to predict that there will be some lock activity soon because a boat has just passed you.

Unless they stop somewhere on route for a picnic, they will eventually reach the next lock and put the water through its paces, so you should be ready for it and cease feeding.

"Blimey mate, I'm too busy trying to catch fish to start charting the progress of boats," I hear you cry. Fair enough, but I think it is all part of the watercraft that will make you a better angler. I'm not saying you have to time the boats or anything that silly, I think you just need to be aware that if a boat has gone past, then you should get ready for the surge that will come. I imagine that a lot of anglers already do this and that they also have that feeling that comes just before the lock opens. There is a moment when the water seems to rise or even flow slightly in the opposite direction before it races off downstream to fill the lock again. So try to be aware of the locks opening and don't feed again until the water has stopped and returned to normal or you will lose fish.

Birds can also become a pest when you are fishing a match. Ducks, drakes, coots and just about every other web-footed creature can make a nuisance of themselves. Don't get me wrong I love birds, especially the one I have for my Christmas dinner, but I just don't want them in my swim when I'm fishing. I don't mind them scuttling about as long as they keep out of my way. I was fishing a river once; stick float down the near side, when a pair of the finest swans you ever did see came gliding up the river. The trouble was that when they got to me, they decided to stop and see if what I was throwing in was any good for eating.

"Go, go on, go go, git out of it," I tried encouraging them as best as I could but all I got in return was some nasty hisses and beating of wings. Did you know a swan could break a man's arm with one swipe? Well everybody else says it, so why shouldn't I.

The only way I could get rid of them was to put my rod down and stop feeding for five minutes. They eventually put their paddles into top gear and scooted off up the river to annoy somebody else. So if there are birds about, don't feed your swim until they've gone, and by this I mean well away. On some occasions, I have waited until a bird gets to what I think is a safe distance from my float only to turn round and come dashing back as soon as the loose feed goes in. You have to watch out for these critters, they swim one way while their eyes are looking in another.

It's not only land locked birds you have to watch out for either. I was once fishing next to a fellow who was having trouble with a seagull. The angler was catching small roach at regular intervals and was being pestered by this bird every time he introduced some loose feed. It would circle round, then drop into his swim, grab some feed and be off again. The whole scenario came to a head when the bird grabbed the next roach the angler hooked as it came to the surface.

"Hey, that's my fish," he shouted as the seagull made off with it. I must admit I'd have used stronger language but there you go. Anyway, the problem was that the fish was still attached to the line so, instead of playing a fish, the angler found himself flying a live kite.

He gave it a little line to start with, but when he realised it might take everything off his reel he gave it a little tug. The result was a seagull that did a fair impression of a kamikaze dive and went straight back into the angler's swim.

The hook had come out of the roach and somehow transferred itself to the bird's beak and it wasn't best pleased. There was lots of squawking as he got it to the net and I'm glad to say it was unhooked successfully and flew off unscathed. The angler however has been scarred for life; he won't feed his swim now if he can so much as hear a bird whistling.

So keep an eye on our feathered friends and enjoy their beauty, but don't chuck any bait in while the greedy little fellows are watching you.

Tip 7: Don't upset the boaters

Boaters and anglers don't get on like a house on fire and that's a fact. This is a shame really because all it would take is a bit of understanding and we could all co-exist quite well.

I know boaters are keen on pointing out that if it wasn't for boats there would be no canals in the first place. But it is also true that, if it wasn't for the revenue provided by anglers, a lot more of them would have been filled in by now. Then the only pleasure the boater would get would be in eating the spuds that had been grown over the top of them.

But it isn't just the canals where tempers can be lost. I saw a very bad case of river rage once on the mighty Severn. This is surprising really because it's a wide piece of water and you'd think there would be enough room for anglers and boaters to live happily together.

The incident happened opposite me on the other bank, so I was what the police would call a first class witness. The fracas was between an angler and a man in a speedboat, and I guess if I had to apportion blame the boater would get it. I'm not being biased you understand, I saw what I saw governor, and that's that.

The trouble erupted when the speedboat went past the angler, pretty close to the bank, causing the angler to shout at the driver.

"You've got the whole pissing river to bugger about on knob-head, why can't you stay out of my swim?"

He shouted it so loud I could hear him across the river, but even so, I expected the speedboater to just carry on his way, but he didn't. He cut his engine revs down to idle and let the current drift him back down to the angler.

"Would you mind repeating that?" he asked the fisherman in a clear posh tone.

"I said, you ought to stick to the middle instead of ruining my swim."

Now I think you'd have to agree that the angler's language was good considering that he had a speedboat hovering over his swim and the driver was revving the engine to keep the boat stationary in the current.

"I'll go where I damn well choose and there's nothing you can do about it," he replied, with a haughty laugh.

"Oh yeah, that's what you think, I'll fix you for ruining my day's fishing," and with that remark, he catapulted a huge pouch full of maggots into the speedboat.

"Bastard," the boater cried, then put the rudder hard over as he opened the throttle. The result was a whirlpool in the angler's swim that was so intense and so deep I could almost see the bottom. He did this for a couple of minutes then was gone up the river, I could still hear him laughing as he went around the next bend.

The moral of the story is this; boaters have the best weapons at their disposal, it's a bit like trying to fight a battle with sticks and stones when your opponent has got an AK47. You are better off making friends with him and trying to get him to see your side of things. After all, most of the problems and bad blood between boaters and anglers are based purely on ignorance.

When the average family books a narrow boat for their well-earned break they don't have anglers in mind. So if their first encounter with them is to find a row of angry looking blokes, who are swearing under their breath and threatening to shower them with maggots, it's no wonder that they get it wrong.

Given the situation I've just described it should come as no surprise that the next time they see a row of anglers their first instinct will be to get past as quick as possible, so they go full steam ahead. They also want to stay as far out of the way as they can, so they steam down the far side where they run aground and have to push the boat off with a bargepole.

So stay calm, give them a little wave and a smile. If nothing else works think about how much money they've wasted for the pleasure of spending a week in a sardine can. And if ever you get the chance to talk to a boater, don't rant at them like a mad man. Tell them quietly and simply that we would prefer it if they could glide slowly and silently down the centre of the canal. While you are telling them, you can always cross your fingers and hope that they sink in the next lock.

Tip 8: Practising is good

When I was an ardent match angler and mentioned to anglers and non-anglers alike that I'd spent the previous evening practising down the canal, I would be greeted with dismay. Practising is something that darts and snooker players do, not anglers. Anglers just turn up, put some bait on their hook, sling it in the water and hope for the best. If you catch a fish it is more to do with luck than anything else, so practising would be a pointless activity.

How wrong can people be? Repeatedly fishing the same venue is a fantastic way to improve your results. Yes I know you can't always fish a water where you've got a match booked, but if you can, you'll find it worth the effort. Top teams wouldn't think of going into a national competition without fishing the water first. They will travel hundreds of miles and stop in a hotel to learn all about the water, so there must be something in it.

It all depends on your circumstances and the importance of the match. Obviously, if you've got a club match booked on a lake sixty miles away and the top prize is likely to be twenty quid it isn't worth it. But at the same time, if the match is going to be fished on a venue that is reasonably close, why not have a couple of sessions and see what you can do.

When I won my local championship, which was held on the Trent and Mersey Canal, for two years in succession, I'm sure that practicing on a regular basis made all the difference. I guess I was also lucky in as much as my wife at the time worked in the evenings and this left me at home with two young sons to look after. But like the Gurus say, if you've got a problem why not turn it into an opportunity and that's what I did. A couple of nights a week, after my wife had left for work, I popped down to the canal taking my kids with me for a few hours. My eldest lad was old enough to fish so I set him up with a pole and the other just sat and watched. We had a laugh and some quality time together but I also got to really know that canal; how the fish responded to various baits and what sort of weights I could attain by trying different methods.

Fishing is no different to any other sport if you want to get better be assured that practicing will help, but, on the other hand, if you want to stay as you are and be pools fodder forever, then that's cool too.

Tip 9: Never give in

Have you ever been halfway through a match and reached the point where it seems that nothing is going right. You've been in a birds nest tangle, missed a succession of bites and knocked your maggot box over. A vale of despondency falls over your whole being and you wonder why you bother. There must be other sports you could do to while away your hours, like snooker, dominoes or darts. These sports have always appealed because you can do them indoors out of the wind, and take a lovely refreshing drink at the same time.

Don't despair, I've been there and as soon as you start catching again, or have a bit of success, life will seem wonderful once more. If I'm not catching I take the time to unwind and relax, sitting in the fresh air in our beautiful countryside is a pleasure in itself. Yeah, I know you are eager to do well in the fishing match and you are probably not bothered about flora and fauna. Well, all I can say is don't give in because matches are often won towards the end when a lot of anglers are thinking about calling it a day.

I suppose I am lucky in that respect because I have done well during several matches when it looked like it was all over and I was going to be an also ran. I remember those successes when I'm in the doldrums and they keep me going right up to the last whistle when others have gone walk about.

The first time it happened was on the river Avon in Warwickshire. This is a river I've never mastered, I don't know why; perhaps it's the trauma of crossing on one of those ferries. Thirty anglers standing up with all their kit in something not much bigger than a park rowing boat, is a real nerve jangler and always gives me a chronic case of the gyp.

I sometimes felt like saying, "I'll wait for it to come back," but my mates would probably have wet themselves laughing. So I always thought of Nelson and Francis Drake and reminded myself that I got my white badge for swimming.

Anyway, the match I was fishing on the day in question was a team match. Each team consisted of three anglers and was done on a section basis, not total weight. The most important thing for a team to do well was to make sure everybody in the team weighed in. This you would think would be easy, but not on a swollen Avon after a hard frost.

For five hours I trotted my stick float down the side. If I tell you that I went from an eighteens and double maggot down to a size twenty-four and a single squatt you will understand how hard it was. By the time three hours had passed, a lot of anglers were walking the bank and chatting. I was informed by those who had already given up and were trying to get some circulation back into their cold feet that hardly anybody was catching. I must admit the thought of jacking in and retiring to the ferry café did cross my mind, not least because I'd have a safer ferry ride on my own. I think the only thing that stopped me was the news that both of my teammates had caught; so if I could just get something on the hook we'd probably be in the frame.

I wasn't hopeful, but I stuck at it and with about twenty minutes to go I was rewarded for my efforts when a stickleback took my bait. That was it for the day but at least we'd all caught so we could be in with a chance.

You can imagine how cold and depressing that day was when I tell you that the scales man was doing the job on his own because most of the anglers had dry nets and they just wanted to get back on the coach or visit the café.

"Have you caught?" He asked when he reached my peg.

"Yes," I replied, "but only a stickleback," and went to pull my keepnet out as usual.

"Don't bother," he said, I'll stick you down for 4 grams is that okay?"

"Yes, I suppose so," I replied, and he was gone.

Now I guess after all these years I'll have to own up to what happened next. When I did drag my net out to empty the stickleback back into the river, he was nowhere to be seen, he must have got through the mesh which was a lot bigger in those days.

Anyway, as it happens, my team came third, we won a trophy each and a small bit of pools money. I kept quiet about there not being a fish in my net, after all it was just a technicality, I had caught the fish, but if the scales man had been doing his job properly I would have registered nil points.

The second time I was rewarded for not giving up was on the river Soar in Leicestershire. On a good day, this river could claim to be marginally better than the Avon if only because most of the fishing is on the same side as the access and therefore, it does not require a ferry crossing to get to your peg. At least you can get off the coach without any fear of being drowned before having a chance to wet your line.

On the day that I am talking about, I drew a peg on a deep bend with a bush overhanging it. There was also a small raft of deadwood that made the whole thing scream "chub," this was going to be a good day I thought optimistically. On my second trot down, just as my float was level with the debris, it sank out of sight. Here comes the first chub of many I thought, but as my rod bent over it didn't feel right. I hadn't seen the fish yet but I knew I'd made a mistake, it wasn't dashing for the nearest snag as chub usually do; it was sort of flapping. Slowly, I managed to bring the fish to the surface and slide the net under a bream weighing about three pounds. Definitely not what I expected but I'll settle for a few more of them thank you very much. We were only five minutes into the match and I'd already got a nice fish in the net so things were looking pretty good.

They say, all good things come to an end and so it was with the fishing that day. You'd think that bream was the last fish in the river because it went as dead as a graveyard. It was soon evident that it wasn't just my swim either and steadily the number of anglers who had succumbed to boredom increased.

"Had out mate?" they'd ask, as they walked past my peg while either scoffing a sandwich or smoking a fag.

"Only the one."

"Lucky bastard, it's more than I've had, I couldn't buy a bite."

It was one of those days the river was not at its best, everybody was saying we were just unlucky; we'd picked a bad day. This is funny because to me it was always the same on this river; you had to work hard to do any good. Today though I would have to admit was worse than usual, and the word on the grape said anybody with over five pounds would skate it.

I of course followed my own advice and stayed at my peg hoping that something would come along. With only about five minutes to go I thought to myself, I could just do with another one of those bream to keep its mate company, and as I did so, the float sank under again and it was another bream, a carbon copy of its mate.

The whistle went almost as soon as I slipped it into the keepnet and I couldn't believe my luck. Those two bream, which could have been identical twins, pushed the scales round to 5lb 10oz and with that I won the match. You're making it up, it's just another fishy story. I can't swallow that load of bull crap I hear you say. Well believe it or not, that is exactly how it happened.

I suppose there would be a few anglers who would claim that catching a good fish in the dying minutes of a match like that was damn lucky. I can go along with that, but only in the same way that anybody who wins the lottery is a lucky spud, but remember that they had to buy a ticket to do it. Those who had packed up fishing early were like the people who hadn't bought a ticket; there was no way they could win.

Tip 10: Keep a bait box lid handy

I don't know about you but there is one creature in this world that I absolutely hate, and that's wasps. Most living things I get on pretty well with, but the dreaded *vespa* is in a league of its own.

It's ironic I suppose that I have never actually been stung, I've come pretty close and I've been attacked by their best but they haven't managed to get me yet. Perhaps that is because I always keep a bait box lid handy on top of my bait waiter. I guess I could take a proper fly swat, but I'd get too many laughs from the hairy bottom brigade.

"Leave them alone and they won't hurt you," is one of those stupid sayings, a lie that rates alongside, "Santa climbing down the chimney" and "the cheque is in the post." I know lots of people who've left them alone and finished up squealing like stuck pigs. No, the best form of defence with a wasp is definitely attack. When they come buzzing in front of you with that side-to-side motion that they make while they're deciding the best place to sting you. Take them by surprise, simply pick up your bait box lid and smack the nasty little beggar as far as you can.

Some people of course have no fear of wasps and my dad was a good example. If a wasp was stupid enough to come into our house, and start climbing the window, my dad would just squash it against the glass with his thumb. The crunching sound is something that I can still remember.

Another angler I know uses wasp grubs for bait and this is something I would actually like to encourage because the sooner wasps are on the endangered species list the better. The angler in question; would make it his business to search out nests in the summer and launch an all out attack on them with a spade. Fair enough I hear you say, but it should be pointed out that he didn't wear any protective clothing. He would make his assault wearing nothing but a pair of jeans, a tee shirt and a pair of good trainers; the latter were essential for running away when the wasps got angry. That is if there is any such thing as a non-angry wasp, they were born with a bad temper.

His method was simple. He would park near to the nest and after eyeing the job up for a bit he would go in with the spade and start digging. It's surprising how much dirt he could shift before the nasty little fellows realised that somebody would have the audacity to do such a thing. Eventually though, the wasps would go on the attack and force him to make a run for it and he'd sprint back to his car to find safety. A few wasps would follow him and look in through the windows and pull nasty faces, but when they realised they couldn't get to him, they'd go back to help build the nest. And what a mess, the poor wasps can't believe humans would do something so horrible. What is it the Queen wasp had told all her children?

"Leave people alone and they won't hurt you." Yeah, it will come as no surprise that wasps tell lies as well.

Anyway, my angling friend repeats the process. He waits for the wasps to calm down a bit, then goes and has a quick dig at the nest before retreating back to his car. After several of these flurries he finally gets what he went after, a bucket full of lovely big soft grubs, chub love them. He swears blind he's never been stung while attacking a nest, but one got him on the neck once when he was lying on his back lawn sunbathing, so I suppose all's fair in love and war.

Another chap I know called Sid, had a way with wasps and I will relate a tale about him to you now. It happened towards the end of a match I was fishing on the Shropshire Union Canal at Norbury Junction. One or two anglers were walking the bank and this fellow was one of them. Now just as he reached me, a big wasp decided he wanted to join my maggots and landed straight in my bait box with them. This took me by surprise and I recoiled a little.

"What's up George?" Sid asked, as he stopped behind me.

"Look at that cheeky bastard," I replied, while pointing to the wasp in my box.

"It won't hurt you if you leave it alone," he said while failing to disguise a chuckle.

"Oh yeah and how am I supposed to get a maggot to put on my hook without disturbing him?" I asked.

"Well you know what I do with wasps don't you?"

"No, you've never told me," I replied. He's told me lots of other stuff but not what he does with wasps.

"I grab their wings behind their back, pick them up and throw them as far as I can."

Now if there was ever a time to call somebody's bluff this was it.

"Okay," I said, "be my guest and show me."

Without any hesitation his hand flashed into my maggot box, he then grabbed the wasp and with a deft flick of the wrist he threw the little monster into the wind.

I have to say I was amazed, but it also left me wondering how he came up with the notion that wasp throwing was a good idea in the first place.

You have probably gathered that I've got a thing about wasps, well I will admit it to the world; yes I have. Have I tried to do anything about it? Yes, I have, and you can read how I got on with my quest to cure my phobia a little later. I have said enough about the rotten little beasties for now, but please remember my tip. Keep a bait box lid handy at all times and do yourself and the rest of us a favour by knocking them all to kingdom come.

Quick tip

Don't take jam sandwiches for your snapping, they will attract every wasp within thirty miles.

Section 4: Just Tales

The final section of this book is about every-day tales and incidents that have happened to me or other anglers while taking part in our chosen sport. Fishing is a wonderful pastime and there is no doubt that it attracts a wide range of characters, some of these and some unique situations have provided me with many happy memories.

Tale 1: Sea fishing

Because I live in the Midlands, the opportunities I have had to go sea fishing have been few and far between. I would also like to be able to say that when the occasion to sample this side of our sport came along that I really enjoyed it, but that would be a fib. I tried it a few times but was left cold and sometimes very sick.

The first time I was supposed to go sea fishing, it never happened. We were taking our annual holiday in our usual resort of Rhyl, and my dad said we could take our rods with us and do some fishing off the beach. I was fourteen years old and looking forward to a change from fishing the local pit, but it wasn't to be, not long after reaching our destination my dad discovered that he'd left our rods leaning against the cooker. Of course I got the blame, hadn't he got enough to do with looking after the cases and everything?

But as it happens all was not lost, he found out that we could take a boat trip and do some proper sea fishing, the rods, bait and all the other necessary tackle would be supplied. This was a lucky break for me, not only would I be introduced to the world of sea fishing, but I'd also be going on a boat, the nearest thing I'd done to sailing before was mucking about in a canoe on the local river.

The following morning I felt a little apprehensive as the boat left the dock with its cargo of a dozen hopeful anglers and as we got further from shore the waves got bigger, the boat started to surge and I began to feel ill. I felt sicker than I'd ever done in my life, this was worse than any fairground ride I'd ever been on. A few people were soon heaving their breakfasts over the side and before long my dad, who up until that point I thought was as tough as old nails, joined in with them.

I suppose we were about a mile from the beach when the skipper cut the motor and we started to drift. If I felt bad before it was nothing to how I felt now, bobbing up and down on the swell was just hell. I thought he must be having a laugh, he'll start the engine again in a minute; no human being could stand feeling so ill for a full hour. Well, the skipper wasn't joking, the engine remained idle and he handed out rods to those who hadn't bought their own with them. He also showed the novices among us how to squeeze the juices out of and then hook a lugworm. This was enough in itself to make one want to puke, but I managed to hold myself together.

It wasn't long before a few mackerel were being caught, and that took my mind off my sickness a bit. I even had a go at dropping my bait over the side, but to be honest my heart wasn't in it because I felt so bad. My father meanwhile, who had by now completely emptied his stomach, was catching a few mackerel and even looked as if he was beginning to enjoy himself, but then it all kicked off. The skipper issued a warning because somebody had just caught a weaver fish. These, he said, contained a vicious poison and shouldn't be touched. Anybody who caught one of these fish should bring it to his attention immediately and he would deal with it. He then held the line above the fish that'd been caught, put it on the gunwale and cut its head off with the biggest and dirtiest sheath knife I'd ever seen. My belly turned over at the sight of this gore, so I glanced over to my dad hoping for a bit of moral support but he was looking the other way and had missed the whole thing.

This was a shame because a few minutes later I caught a dreaded weaver fish. I was just swinging it in to my hand when my dad grabbed it as if it was a small roach. I guess he thought he was doing me a favour with me looking so sick, but he soon wished he hadn't bothered.

"Christ all flaming mighty," and a host of other words mostly starting with the letter f, poured from his throat in an unending torrent as the barb on the back of the fish's head sank into the palm of his hand.

It didn't help matters that the skipper's first instinct was to wade in without a hint of sympathy.

"I've just bloody warned everybody on the boat about the weaver fish, I said, I'd deal with the bloody things."

"Well I didn't hear you," my dad said, "I've been deaf as a post in one ear since the war."

On hearing this excuse, the skipper softened and was so concerned about my dad's welfare that he cut the trip ten minutes short so that he could get him back to dry land to see a doctor. The rest of the anglers on the boat could have moaned but they all seemed to be relieved that the ordeal we'd been through was over.

My father went to the doctors and was given some pills and we then went to meet my mum. He told her when the fish stung him it was like having a bolt of lightning go up his arm which by now had swollen to twice its normal size. It took a couple of days for him to get better but I'm afraid my view of sea fishing had been spoilt for life.

My next encounter with sea fishing didn't happen until I was sixteen and living on the other side of the world. My father had come home from work one night and announced to the family that we were going to emigrate to Australia and that is what we did.

To be truthful, fishing as I knew it was non-existent because it was sea fishing or nothing. Now when I say sea fishing it wasn't quite the same as the trip in Rhyl. Sea fishing in Australia was a lot cruder than it was in Wales, but that shouldn't come as a surprise to anybody.

The tackle was simple; some ten pound breaking strain line, a size eight hook and a big lump of lead.

Sorry there is one other essential item in an Ozzy angler's tackle bag, an empty coke bottle. I sometimes wonder how the world of fishing would cope without the coke bottle.

Where's the rod? I hear you ask. Well there wasn't one. The coke bottle took the place of the rod and the reel. The line was wrapped around the bottle and the hook and weight were attached in the traditional way.

To cast out, the bottle was held in one hand with the open end roughly pointing towards where you wanted your terminal tackle to land. The other hand gripped the line two yards (a couple of metres) up from the lead; this was then twirled around the head, pretty much following the style of a South American bolas thrower. Once enough momentum had been gained you let go and hoped that it went in the right direction, many did not.

Once the weight settled on the seabed, the line was tightened by wrapping any spare around the bottle, which was then put on the ground in an upright position. The anglers would then stand and stare at the bottle and wait for it to topple over. This was the Ozzy anglers' only method of bite detection.

The actual fishing I was involved in took place on a pier in the docks area of Melbourne called Williamstown. We used whitebait for bait and caught sea bream and snapper, nothing of any size. My brother laid claim to the biggest fish I saw caught, a banjo shark weighing about 12 pounds, but even that didn't put up much of a fight. I guess the best part of the fishing was not landing the fish, but trying to catch a hold of your coke bottle as it scuttled around the ground when a good fish took your bait.

My dad soon discovered that Australia wasn't going to be the place of his dreams. It wasn't the flies or the hot weather that got him down it was the beer. Not that there wasn't enough, (rumour has it that some of the natives shower in it every day) the whole drinking culture was wrong.

The facts are that there aren't many pubs in Australia, so most people drink at other peoples' houses while they have a barby. My dad missed the oak beams, a game of dominoes and a pint in a pint glass. He also missed real beer; he reckoned they didn't have brewers in Australia, just chemists.

For the record, I became home sick much quicker than the rest of the family and, when I was eighteen, I returned to England leaving my parents and siblings out there. They did eventually follow me home after my father had saved enough money for the tickets.

Sea fishing didn't raise its head again for a few years, but then a bloke where I worked decided to organise a sea fishing trip. Jack, as he was called, went around the factory trying to raise some enthusiasm and enlist enough people to fill a mini bus. He was full of tales of sea fishing, the trips he'd been on and the fish he'd caught. I didn't fancy it; my experience at Rhyl still loomed large in the back of my mind whenever I was within earshot of a sea gull's scream. Eventually though, I gave in and decided I'd go. The weather would probably be a lot kinder than it was in Wales, I told myself.

Well it wasn't, the sea roared and the boat tossed us about something chronic and we were all as sick as mops. We were after all just a bunch of landlubbers, pretending to be sea anglers, so it wasn't a surprise that we were all proper poorly. When I say all I mean with the exception of Jack, he wasn't sick at all. Now don't imagine he was hauling in fish like a deep-sea trawler man and grinning at the rest of us, because he wasn't.

Jack, you see, had a method for avoiding sea sickness that had been passed on to him by Gary, an angler who told tall stories with a face as straight as a poker. Unfortunately, Gary couldn't come with us on the trip but he passed his wisdom on to us should the weather turn out rough. Anyway, it did turn out to be rough and Jack decided as soon as he started feeling queasy that he would take the advice given by Gary. He lay on his back so that his spine was centred over the keel and stretched out his arms as if he was going to be crucified. He lay there for most of the trip and how he managed to avoid being trampled is still a mystery to me.

The other thing that struck me was that one of Gary's tales turned out to be true, because with the exception of the skipper and Jack everybody managed to turn their stomachs inside out. This left me wondering about the validity of his other stories, so I will relate a couple of them to you in a later chapter and let you make your mind up for yourself.

Anyway the sea fishing trip wasn't much fun for Jack, lying on his back in the middle of a boat for four hours. It wasn't exactly a bundle of laughs for me either, so I've never had even the slightest urge to go sea fishing again. If ever I show any signs of weakness you have my permission to hunt me down and clobber me with a wet cod.

Tale 2: My first success

Yes, I'm still writing about fishing. I was going through the loft the other day and found my little box of treasures. It contained some old photographs, a pen knife with a broken blade, some foreign coins and that sort of thing. In the middle was a memento from the first thing I ever won in a fishing match. Not a lovely gilded trophy with a fake marble base, or even a bronze medal, no, this was the top off a beer bottle; a bottle of Man's Brown Ale to be precise.

It was a fur and feather match and I came ninth; it was a shame that last roach came off at the net, because the next prize up the list was a bottle of Guinness. Still you can't have everything.

When I picked the top up and felt its jagged edge I expected all sort of memories to come flooding back. What method and bait I'd used, what sort of fish I'd caught and my total weight, but there was almost nothing, that is with the exception of the ferry.

I've already described how the ferries on the river Avon give my nerves some grief. Well this was my first actual encounter with a ferry and it was on the river Trent at a place called Farndon. If anything, this ferry was smaller than anything on the Avon but it still held a coach full of anglers. I might not be able to remember the fishing, but the fear of being plunged into that icy river on a cold November morning will never leave me, even if I live to be a hundred and ten.

Tale 3: Some funny folk go fishing

We all have our idiosyncrasies but I suppose fishing boasts an enormous variety when compared with other sports. If you look at one golfer you've probably seen them all, they all look the same and act the same.

Don't get me wrong, I'm not having a dig at golfers they're a grand bunch of chaps and I know a lot of them are also maggot drowners. My point is that they all dress and act the same, which is not true of our sport.

One day, I took some time off work to go fishing and decided that a small farm pool would suit me fine. When I got there at about six o'clock I had the whole pool to myself, which was very nice because like I said, it's pretty small. In fact, it's so small that the total number of pegs it held was four.

There was the one where I chose to fish and three at the other end. The bank opposite me was a straight six-foot drop to the water, so nobody ever fished there. This was just as well because I was sitting on one side and casting the short distance to this opposite bank.

After a couple of hours, I was just counting on having the place to myself for the day when I saw another car coming across the field. Ah well, not to worry, I thought; there's room down the other end, they won't disturb me. But as soon as the three stooges got out of their car I had a feeling I was in for trouble.

Remember me telling you about the high bank with the six-foot vertical drop straight down to the water, the one opposite me, below which up until three minutes ago was where I'd been putting my float. Well not anymore, because this is where they chose to set up. They totally ignored me as if I didn't exist. I of course had to change where I was casting to and build up a new swim, I thought of moving altogether but I couldn't be bothered and I just hoped the three stooges wouldn't be any bother once they'd set up.

To be honest, I was also curious about these people because they looked as if they would provide better entertainment than the fishing. It was as if they'd come straight from the planet Zog and our atmosphere was playing havoc with their co-ordinations. They moved about like eighty year-old men but none of them looked a day over forty. And they were dressed kind of strange for anglers. If I say they were wearing the suits they'd probably worn for their Sunday best twenty years earlier, you might get some idea. One of them, the man who sat in the middle, was even wearing a pair of white brogues.

I looked at these three anglers, I will call them that for want of a better word, but I don't think they were proper anglers. They sat in a row on the high bank with their rods sticking up at forty-five degree angles because they only had one rod rest each. The butt ends of their rods rested on the ground while at the other end the thick line came from their rod tips in curls that were reminiscent of a pig's tail. If this wasn't bad enough, the curly line led to three floats that were big enough to warn a sailor of rocks ahead. I dread to think what their hooks looked like, but I doubted they were smaller than a tens.

So as I sat there fishing, I also watched and listened to these people and became fascinated with them. Perhaps they'd escaped from an institution. Considering they were all sat together on that big bank I guess they didn't say much really, well not until it happened. The one in the middle, you remember him the one wearing the brogues. He stood up, took a couple of paces forward with a handful of something to feed his swim, but as he threw it in he sort of forgot to let go. He went straight into the water doing the belly flop of all belly flops.

I could hardly believe it, he sort of twisted round in the water looking as if he was trying to stand up and do the doggy paddle at the same time. Whatever he was doing it propelled him to the bank where he grasped wildly at clumps of grass in an effort to extricate himself from the water. Such was the commotion you'd think a crocodile had grabbed one of his legs.

Throughout this episode, there was one thing that struck me. I expected his two friends to come to his aid but they never even moved a muscle. They just sat there looking at their floats as if they were about to get a bite at any minute. Eventually, the one on the right spoke to the man in the water.

"I told you that you should've worn your wellies didn't I?"

This was just about the driest quip I'd ever heard and because I knew I'd be unable to control my hysteria for much longer, I packed up and went home to find some sanity.

Little Hitlers, I suppose all sports have them and fishing has more than most. Give these officious bastards a little power and it goes straight to their heads. I went to a match one afternoon and only six other anglers turned up, even the match secretary hadn't made it and he had the scales. If it had been any other day I wouldn't have bothered, but it was a Saturday and I knew that if I'd gone home I'd have finished up going out shopping. I don't know about you, but I'd sooner fish an empty ditch than go to the shops.

So the seven of us, including the stand in match secretary, decided to give it a go and, to be honest, it wasn't much better than fishing a mucky bath because very little was caught. Three hours of wishing was what it amounted to, and dreams of days when the water was really producing. Still, we'd all caught a few bits, so it was going to be a close thing.

The weigh in would be exciting because we were fishing for the pools money and I, like most of the other anglers, assumed that with such a small turn out, it would be a case of winner takes all. We'd all stuck £3 in the kitty so the winner would get £21, not bad for an afternoon's sport and much better than going shopping.

The stand in match secretary however, saw things differently, but first we had to go through the farce of a weigh-in. Now if you recall the official match secretary with his precision calibrated scales had not shown up, so Mr Standin decides to do the job with his landing net and a set of rusty Samsons that he must have had for a father's day present twenty years ago.

As it happens there was no argument about the winner, he had what looked like about a pound and a half of fish and that's roughly what the scales showed. Behind him came two anglers who registered 10 ounces each and after that came yours truly and Mr Standin, we both registered 8 ounces. The two bringing up the rear had 5 and 3 ounces each.

So like I said before, we all expected the £21 to go to the winner and that is what he expected too, but Mr Standin had his own set of rules and was paying out differently. His decision was obviously influenced by the fact that he came a joint third with me.

We all argued with him and said he was being silly but he wouldn't have it, he was paying 1st, 2nd and 3rd as usual. The fact that it was only like that because his crappy scales were unable to differentiate between the weights didn't bother him, or the fact that he would be paying out five anglers in a field of seven. In the end the winner had £12, the two anglers in joint 2nd place had £3 each, while me and Mr Standin, had thirty bob a piece.

This was the only time my winnings were less than I'd paid in pools money, but it does prove that this world and angling produces some very strange folk.

Tale 4: The challenge

I know boxers have to put up with it all the time. You can picture the champ down the local having a sip of pop when some knucklehead, who's had too much apple crush, decides he wants to fight him. Apparently, it happens all the time and it happened to me. No, he didn't want a fight, but he'd heard I was pretty handy with the rods and he challenged me to a match, head to head, one to one. Paul was his name and he was even willing to bet me a fiver that he could beat me.

I gave it a little bit of thought, because he could've just been pulling my leg. I knew him pretty well because he'd been a regular in the same pub as me for a number of years. He worked on a farm somewhere and was a hard working sort, who liked his beer.

I also knew that Paul wasn't always flush with cash because of the story about him and a vet that was often peddled around the pub when people wanted to wind him up, which was quite often. Paul, so the story goes, had a springer spaniel bitch that was about to give birth and make him a few bob. Anyway like I said, he didn't have much money so when the vet turned up, he told him he couldn't pay him, but he could have first pick of the litter by way of payment. Well after a lot of yelping the bitch only had one puppy, and the vet went home with it.

Knowing this, I declined his challenge as I felt sorry for him, but he was insistent and started calling me chicken, so I offered to meet him down the canal on Sunday morning.

"I'm not fishing the poxy canal," he declared, "too many boats. There's a nice little pond on the farm, we can fish that, it's full of fish."

"I suppose you've fished it before?"

"Yeah loads, but that shouldn't bother a crack angler like you should it?"

"No it doesn't, but are you sure you want to risk a fiver on it."

"I've never been more sure in my life, it'll be nice to make some easy money for a change."

Well what could I do? I was certain I could beat this loud mouth even though he did have a territorial advantage. But then the rest of the pub joined in with his cajoling of me so the bet was on.

On the morning of the match I picked him up and he gave me directions to the pool. We established some rules on the way and agreed on it being a three-hour match. We would then adjourn to the pub where the loser could buy a round of drinks and hand over the fiver in front of the regulars.

We soon arrived at the pool; well duck pond would be a better description. It was very small, it had reeds at one end and a few hawthorn bushes dotted around the perimeter. It was of a similar shape and about the same size as a tennis court.

I had hardly stopped the car when Paul jumped out and scuttled off around to the other side to what was obviously his favourite peg. Not that there were any proper pegs, I think he was the only one who fished it. In contrast, I took a leisurely look at the water and gave some thought to where I was going to fish from, while he was setting up like a demon. I soon found out why, as soon as he'd tackled up he started fishing. I of course protested that we should both start together but he said he hadn't got time to wait while I farted about the place.

This jelled me into action and I set up almost opposite him and a little way towards the reeds. My guess was that this was the shallower water and, with it being warm, this is where the fish were most likely to be. From this position I could also keep an eye on how the opposition was performing.

I went straight in with the punched bread, as I assumed that like all farm ponds it would be full of stunted fish. I was right and on my very first cast I hooked a small roach. This was one nil to me because although he'd been fishing for at least ten minutes I hadn't seen him catch anything. I won't bore you with the details but it didn't go well for Paul. After a couple of hours the bites were starting to fade for me too so I told Paul I was going to have to change bait.

"Are you changing to bread?" he asked.

"No, I've been on bread all morning I'm going onto maggots now," I replied.

"How many have you caught?" he asked.

"One hundred and twenty six; how about you?"

"Twelve," he said dourly, "come on let's pack up, I've had enough." As he said it, he tossed what was left of his bait into the water, so the subject obviously wasn't up for discussion.

Not a word was spoken on the way to the pub but he made up for it when he got there. He told those present that he'd never seen anything like it and he didn't know it was possible to catch fish so quickly. He was kind in defeat, while I was flattered and I enjoyed the roar when he handed over the fiver.

A couple of pints later I quietly slipped it back into his hand, after all, I'd had some reasonable sport that morning and that was good enough for me.

Tale 5: Piking

I guess that fishing for pike is slightly better than sea fishing because at least you are on dry ground. But in my opinion it hasn't got much going for it.

Firstly, pike fishing is mostly done in the cold weather when most other fish are lying doggo on the bottom. Secondly, pound for pound the pike puts up about the same fight as a wet dishcloth. I know dishcloths can't fight, and that's the point I'm making, neither can a pike.

Still, I've had a go and I've caught a few including a couple in double figures, but they didn't fill me with joy. In fact, I hated getting the hooks out because I was always a bit fearful of being savaged by those razor sharp teeth.

Most of the piking I've done was with dead bait, sardines and whitebait being my favourites. Call me a sissy if you want but I never fancied live baiting, as I would empathise too strongly with the victim. I've also had some success with spinning but I found it a bit like fly fishing, a hell of a lot of effort for very little reward.

I think one of the reasons I don't like piking is because these fish are so stupid. In fact, I like to think that pike mirror our society perfectly. The majority of the population is made up of nice gentle people, but there are a few nasty folk about who think they can solve any problem with violence. These vicious people are like pike because they too, are intellectually challenged.

Yes I know all you pike lovers will be jumping up and down now, and want to smash something, but just calm down a minute and consider the facts. I've seen photos of a pike that was so stupid it choked while trying to swallow another pike that was much bigger than itself. This is the dining equivalent of you trying to swallow a sumo wrestler.

You may still have doubts about the intelligence of the average pike, so here is a little tale. I was walking around a small pool one winter's morning, flicking out a spinner here and there to see if I could tempt any predators, be they pike or perch. Now I'll have to admit that I wasn't going about it in a fully focused way because I finished up casting my spinner into the bottom branches of a tree, that overhung an inlet where I'd just cast. I tried to retrieve it by shaking and jiggling it, but in the end I had to resort to the only way known to man. I put my rod down and pulled like hell on the line.

You've guessed it; the line broke leaving the spinner dangling about six inches above the water and a nasty trap for any moorhens or ducks. While I pondered the best way to get around to this tree and find a method to retrieve my end tackle something very silly happened. A pike weighing about two pounds jumped up out of the water and hung itself on my spinner.

I stood back for a moment unable to believe what I was seeing. The fish was thrashing its tail about causing a commotion and its obvious distress motivated me to get around to it as fast as possible. As I went round to the inlet there was a satisfying plop and thanks to my barbless hooks, Percy Pike had managed to wriggle off the spinner and drop back into the water. What a relief, I thought, now all I have to do is a bit of tree climbing and get my tackle back. I guess I was half way through the tree and just coming to the place where it overhung the water when Percy showed up again and on his very first attempt managed to hang himself on my trebles for the second time. Again there was a lot of splashing, but just before I managed to get the landing net under him he managed to break free again. I still couldn't believe what I'd just seen and I grabbed my spinner as quickly as possible before he did an encore. Having witnessed this event I can only say that I'm convinced that the pike must be the daftest fish on the planet.

Before we leave the issue of pike, I reckon that this fish is mentioned most often in tall fishing stories. Well, a couple of chapters ago, I mentioned a chap called Gary, who had a reputation for telling a tall story. I will recall a couple for you now and you can decide if they are true or not. Remember though that he tells them with a straight face and you can't laugh, because he is adamant that every word is true.

On the fishing front, he was always telling me about the big one that got away, and the enormous pike that lived in a special pool that only he had permission to fish. He said he was approaching the water one day and stepped on what he thought was a log at the side. But this log happened to be one of the water's big pike and it took off with Gary on its back. He reckoned he surfed at least half-way across the pool on it before he fell off.

He was also a keen motorcyclist, and one day he told me about a scary experience he'd had when riding his motorbike on a trip through Wales. Apparently, he had been stuck in traffic for some time and getting frustrated, so he decided to open it up and pass a line of slow moving vehicles. He was going very fast and didn't realise that a corner was coming up and there wouldn't be enough time to slow down. So what could he do? Well there was only one thing for it. Using the kerb as a launch ramp, he flipped the bike up into the air and leaned it into the crash barrier that went around the bend. His wheels went into the centre channel and he rode the barrier right to the end where he plopped off back on to the road as cool as a polar bear's cock. This apparently all happened at ninety miles an hour, now what do you reckon, porky or what?

Quick Tip

When spinning for pike and sport is slow, try putting a sardine or whitebait onto the spinner it often attracts a take almost immediately.

Tale 6: Booze and chips

I know that a lot of people put fishing and boozing together like strawberries and cream but I don't believe the majority of anglers mix the two pleasures. There may be a few anglers, who put a bottle of Chardonnay in the stream to cool before they commence fishing, but these are most likely to be game fisherman and probably live in Canada. Having a bottle of wine soaking at the side of the Trent and Mersey doesn't seem quite the same.

I also know that a good few of you may pop into the local and a have couple when you've finished a session but it's not often and the reasons are simple.

Firstly, the end of your fishing session does not coincide with the best time for you to go and get hammered.

Secondly, you don't want to go for a drink because you've been bagging up all day and you are knackered.

Thirdly, you smell, not horrendous but you have acquired the odour of a newly opened can of mackerel and, as such, could attract some unwanted glances.

Fourthly and perhaps the most important reason is that you are expected to arrive home at a certain time. It may not be written down, but you know when it is and so does she. Of course you wear the waders in your house, but you're a reasonable sort of guy, you've spent most of the weekend doing what you love doing while she's been catching up on the housework. So you act fairly and go home because it's the right thing to do. Plus, if you play fairly, she won't mind you going again next week, and the costly divorce will be put off for a little while longer.

The strangest recollection I have of mixing fishing and booze was in the late seventies. I had a national match coming up on the Grand Union Canal near Northampton. I had never fished this canal before and neither had one of my mates Simon, so we decided we'd have a practice session and he offered to drive.

Anyway, a few days before we went, another lad called Darryl who works in the same factory as us, asked Simon if he could come with us. It's a big factory and we didn't know this person, but sharing the cost of petrol seemed a good idea so he'd said okay.

We picked this lad up, I say lad he must have been about twenty-five years old and around six foot tall. He had long, dark-black hair and a bandanna around his forehead, which made him look like Geronimo, but other than that he looked like the rest of us. The trip was long and on the way there Simon and I engaged in our usual banal banter and tried our best to bring Geronimo into the conversation. However, he just uttered a few words and I think he said "ugh," every now and again, but it wasn't very often.

Eventually, we reached the Canal and Simon and I set up on adjacent pegs. We expected our Indian friend to go on the next one because they all looked the same, but he missed one out and went on the next. Was it something we said? I don't think so, he was just one of life's loners and as long as he couldn't get his hands on a bow and a quiver full of arrows, I'm sure we'd be all right.

The fishing was slow, a few roach and gudgeon were all we were catching and this was when we noticed that Geronimo was bending his elbow in another way. Every now and again there would be a tisssh sound and when we looked in his direction he'd be opening another can of ale.

"He can't have brought much tackle with him," Simon said, as we packed up for the day, "he must've drunk at least twenty cans of beer since we got here."

"Yeah," I agreed, "but he still managed to catch as much as us, I think I might bring my own barrel next time I fish this place."

The drive home was uneventful with just two of us doing all the talking. I was tired and a nap would have been nice but I was too frightened that Simon might drop off as well. So to break the journey up we stopped about halfway to stretch our legs and get some fish and chips. Well that's what Simon and I bought, we met Geronimo back at the car; he hadn't got any chips just a couple of six packs of Guinness.

The rest of the journey home was punctuated to the sound of tisssh as the brave warrior ripped the ring pulls from another succession of cans.

Tale 7: A night to remember

Fishing follows fashion just like every other walk of life. I'm not talking clothes here as much as fads and fancies. When I started fishing there was no such thing as a boily, but suddenly they were everywhere and everybody was using them. They are still popular and can be purchased in a variety of flavours but they are out of fashion when compared with pellets and other more exotic baits.

Dog biscuits were all the rage once, then cat food and most anglers found themselves reading the angling press just in case there was a new sensation in the offing. It was just after one of these new ideas had appeared in print that Tony, one of my best fishing buddies, and I set off on a night fishing trip to a nearby mere. The water was gaining a reputation amongst specimen hunters because it had recently produced some very big bream that were close to breaking the record.

We'd fished the water before and although we'd taken some big tench and here I'm talking fish over five pounds, we didn't fish it often because it was hard. Now when I say hard, I don't just mean hard in terms of trying to get a bite, I mean hard in every other sense. The water is relatively shallow, and like all meres this means that it has a thick fringe of reeds around the perimeter. The fishing is done from a small number of wooden jetties that go out beyond the reed line.

Extreme care was always required because these jetties consisted of just a few posts with planks nailed on the top. Don't get me wrong, they were probably great when they were first put up, but when we fished there, they were well on their way to being rotten. Getting to the jetty was also a nightmare. First you had to negotiate a barbed wire fence, then a wood full of thick undergrowth, which isn't easy when you are loaded with tackle. After emerging from the wood you are confronted with a series of planks that lead you to the rotten jetty. I know it doesn't sound much fun but even anglers like a bit of adventure now and again, plus we might become record breakers before dawn.

And so it was that just before dark, we found ourselves safe and relieved to have made it onto the jetty just in time to set up for the night. There wasn't a breath of wind, or any sign of rain, which was just as well because there was nowhere to stick a brolly in, and once seated it would have been foolish to move again before first light. It wouldn't be possible to get back onto dry land safely that night, so we were going to have to make the best of it no matter what happened.

If you remember earlier on in this book I advised against letting anybody else supply you with bait. In that instance I was talking about match fishing, but if you follow this story you will find that it's appropriate at all times.

Like I said, we'd set up just in time because the light was beginning to fade.

"Where's the bait?" I asked Tony.

He bent down to his bag and fetched out a bag of brown breadcrumb and four and a half pint boxes of maggots.

"The half pint is for the hook," he said, "the others are for mixing in with the ground bait."

"What's the difference?" I asked.

"I've blanched them," he said, with a big smile and an air of authority.

"Blanched them, what the hell does that mean? I've never heard of blanched maggots. What's so special about blanched maggots?"

"You'll see when you take the lid off," he said and boy was he right, talk about a shock to the senses.

The smell was overpowering. I used to live near an animal processing plant, that burnt dead cows, sheep and the like, and that is exactly how these maggots smelt. It was a warm putrid stench and made me gag. Besides the smell the sight of these maggots was enough to turn anybody's stomach. Long, stretched out and lifeless, they were dead, stinking to high heaven and we had half a gallon of them.

"What the hell have you done to them?" I asked.

"Blanched them," was the reply, "I saw it in the angling paper, somebody recommended it. I put the maggots in a bucket and poured a kettle full of boiling water over them. Pong a bit don't they?"

"Pong, they flaming well wreak, and you still haven't told me why."

"It's to stop them crawling away in the night, it'll be too dark to keep feeding bait in, we'll have it all over the place. All we've got to do is mix the maggots with the breadcrumb and chuck half of it in. We can throw the rest in later."

"Well there you go then Mr Blancher," I said to him, as I handed him my share of the maggots. "It'll be bad enough me having to share this jetty with half a bucket of them without getting the stink on my hands."

"Fair enough," he said, and complied with my request without debate. He mixed the stuff up in the bucket and threw half the contents into the water. I guess we must have stuck it out for a hour and in that time blanched maggots had failed to bring us a single bite. The smell, however, did manage to attract a huge cloud of midges and mosquitoes. On top of that the pong was getting unbearable, so the rest of the contents of the bucket went into the mere before midnight.

I'm pretty sure the fish couldn't stand the smell either because we didn't have a sniff of a bite all night. I say all night, we didn't really stay all night. As soon as it was light enough, we packed up and headed to a small pool close by and there we had some good sport without the need for a single blanched maggot.

Tale 8: He wore it well

Most anglers I know aren't bothered about fashion, but they are extremely concerned about comfort. Some anglers will carry on fishing through the winter months and want to keep warm, so they invest heavily in special clothing. Colin Brown was one of these guys.

He kept an eye on trends and what was available to those who enjoyed the great outdoors. Colin was one of the first anglers in our neck of the woods to wear the boots they use in cold storage facilities to keep his feet warm. He was also one of the first anglers around our way to adopt the one-piece suit. He took a lot of stick at the first match he turned up to, as anglers thought he was wearing a big baby's romper suit. But when they saw how warm he was at the end of a match a lot of them copied him.

It wasn't long after the one-piece suit became standard wear for a lot of anglers that Colin went a step further and got a new one that had a built in hood. I was there the day he christened it on the river Nene. A cold blustery day it was in the sad old month of November, and Colin found himself in need of a toilet. Apparently, he'd eaten something iffy the night before. Anyway, he passed a friend of mine and went behind a couple of bushes to do his business.

He emerged a couple of minutes later, obviously pleased with himself and stopped to speak to my friend. Firstly to enquire how well he was catching, and seeing that my friend looked cold he probably also wanted to show off his new ensemble.

"Catching much?" he enquired of my friend, who was by now turning to see who it was.

"A few bits, nothing big," he answered, at the same time as he saw it was Colin, smiling smugly as ever.

"Yeah, tough isn't it," Colin said, pleased that he'd got the angler's attention. "The secret is keeping warm," he said, as he flipped his hood over his head. As soon as he'd done it, the pan full of sloppy jumbos that he'd just done behind the bushes, slithered down the front of his face and into his beard.

The day Colin crapped in his own hood will never be forgotten, and in some parts he is still known as Shithead Brown.

Tale 9: Time to get a watch

You put it off for as long as you can, but life is peppered with those occasions when you have to raise the white flag. You surrender, it's time to give in and join the rest of the human race. Technology is often to blame because it moves so fast.

I was very late in getting BBC2 because it meant shelling out for a new aerial. I was also late getting colour. The same goes for video recorders, DVD players and mobile phones. So if I tell you that I was in my mid-twenties before I purchased my first watch, you probably wouldn't be a bit surprised.

So there I was, about twenty-five years old and about to set the match fishing world on fire. On the day of my first match, I was so excited that I double-checked my bait and tackle to make sure I had everything I needed for my debut. Then it hit me, how was I going to tell the time without a watch? Surely I'd need to have some idea about how much of the match was left. There wouldn't be any clocks hanging about down the canal and I couldn't keep shouting to the bloke on the next peg to ask him the time could I?

Resourceful as ever; I soon came up with a cracking solution to the problem. I dug out my good old, Big-Ben repeater clock, the one that my wife had made me replace with a new radio alarm. I set it to the correct time, wound it up and stuck into my tackle box. During the match everything was ticking along nicely and I guess we were about halfway through when the peace and quiet was broken by the alarm on my clock going off and shattering the silence. I almost fell in the cut as the ringing demon went off right under my bum. But the embarrassment was even worse, hundreds of eyes focused on me from all along the towpath in both directions.

I switched it off as quickly as I could, but my face was still red when the scales came round. Other anglers were of course only too pleased to have a bit of fun at my expense.

"What time is it?" asked Joe.

"I don't know Joe," replied Jim."

"Have you any idea Peter?"

"No, I need to get a little hand put on this watch," he replied, mimicking Hilda Baker.

"How about you George, surely you know what time it is?"

"Yeah yeah, very funny, I know, it's time I got a watch. Following this incident I did actually get a watch, but I still can't get used to wearing one, it's the last thing I put on before going out of the house, and the first thing I take off on my return.

Tale 10: It's an ill wind

In a previous chapter I talked about making your own floats, if you try it please be careful because they do become quite precious. I was fishing a large pond one windy afternoon in autumn, and catching one or two roach. Nothing fantastic, but interesting enough to keep me there in what were not the most pleasant of conditions.

There were only two other anglers present on that afternoon and they shared a peg on the opposite side. I don't know what it is about some anglers, but if they're not sitting on their mate's lap they aren't happy. These two were only separated by a small clump of weeds and with their strange woolen hats they put me in mind of the flowerpot men. Personally, I like to spread out and get my money's worth. Day tickets don't come cheap anymore; I could have belonged to six clubs a few years ago for the sort of cash that I'm now paying out for a single session. Still the fishing is much better so I shouldn't complain.

Anyway, back to the pond I was telling you about. During the afternoon, I got snapped, but not on the hook length where you usually expect it, for some reason the line parted just above the float. This was then left bobbing about on the water.

Now you may recall that the conditions that day were windy or what the weather girl might call blustery. I know there are many experts who say that when it's windy you should always fish with your face into the wind. Apparently, this is because all the fish will be following wind-blown food and congregating along that bank. I reckon this is only so that the experts can have the nice calm pegs on the other side all to themselves. I hate fishing with the wind in my face and, given the choice, I'd sooner sit in comfort and catch a few fish, rather than endure hours of misery while hoping for a few more.

So on that windy day I picked a peg with the wind firmly behind me, whereas the two anglers opposite were obviously of the other persuasion and chose to fish into the wind. The only problem for me now was the retrieval of my float. It was now minus the shot that was on the line, so it was sitting a little higher in the water. In fact, it was quite easy to see as it drifted with the wind towards Bill and Ben, who hadn't yet spotted its approach.

I kept my eye on it and finally it entered Ben's swim.

"Hey up, what's that bobbing about?" Asked Bill.

"Looks like a float," said Ben, "I'm having that bugger," and with that comment he got up with his landing net and tried to reach my float. But even with it fully extended he still came up short.

"Why don't you have some patience and wait a minute. It's coming your way and it will be in the side soon," Bill advised.

Ben ignored him and stepped out into the water as far as his wellies would allow. He tried again, but still couldn't reach.

"I told you, you'd be better waiting a bit. You're disturbing the fish with that landing net," said Bill, who was now getting frustrated by his friend's obsession.

"Look Bill," Ben said, "I'm having that float now, you know what the wind is like round these parts it can change in a flash, then I'd be right up crap creak without a paddle."

He then grabbed the bunch of weeds and leaned forward as far as he could.

"Ah shit," he declared.

"What's up now?" Bill asked sharply.

"The bloody water's gone over the front of me welly."

However, he was undeterred and after a final swish he caught his prize. Now, my first thoughts were to walk around the bank and ask for it back but I decided against it. As it happens it was the right decision because as Ben took the float out of his landing net and examined it with a critical eye, he said, "All that for a bit of bloody home-made crap." He then snapped it in half and threw it into the bushes behind him.

Tale 11: A bit more about wasps

I think I made it clear in an earlier chapter that I don't get on with wasps at all. It's therefore ironic that they should be so attracted to me and all I can do is keep batting them into the water with my bait box lid.

I have tried to cure myself of waspitus and once sat in a conservatory with a wasp for five minutes while it searched out every inch of the windows looking for an escape route. The door of course was wide open, but the dozy creature couldn't work it out. It buzzed and buzzed and finally rattled my nerves so badly that I splattered it across the glass with a rolled up copy of the local newspaper. I was pretty pleased with myself afterwards because to spend five minutes in the same room as a wasp was a real achievement for me. I usually shout a bit and smack them with the nearest object as soon as they appear.

It wasn't long after this attempt at self-curing my phobia that an evening match came up on one of my favourite venues. It was a club match on a lovely little thirty pegger that always fishes well. I'd practiced there a few times during the last couple of weeks in preparation for this match and the fishing was good. The only downside, as I saw it, was the fact that just to the left of peg two, which is one of the better spots, a gang of wasps had decided to make a nest. Still, as long as I didn't draw that peg everything would be all right.

As we gathered on the night in question, waiting for all the anglers to arrive for the draw, I told everybody about the wasp's nest on peg two. My hope was that with their help we could lobby the match secretary to take it out. But it was no good because my plan didn't work. Match anglers can be apathetic at the best of times, and the organizer, quite frankly, didn't give a shit.

Yeah, I know you are one step ahead of me and of course I drew peg two. But I'm British, and like the great Earnest Shackleton, I wouldn't be deterred from my endeavours. That night, my need to win that match was stronger than my fear of being stung. Well it was when we were still in the car park, but when I got to the water and saw all those nasty things in their black and yellow jumpers I nearly freaked out. At that point I could've turned around and gone home but something pushed me on. Perhaps I was scared of the ribbing I'd get from my fellow anglers or perhaps I was just being stubborn, but I stayed.

The secret is not to rile them, I said to myself. They are busy little creatures going about their business; if I don't bother them, they won't bother me. I put my tackle down slowly and set my rod up well away from the entrance to their nest. While I was doing this, an odd wasp or two would come to have a look at me out of curiosity and to see if I'd got any jam sandwiches.

I refrained from lashing out with the old bait box lid and spoke to them quietly.

"Go along there nice Mr Waspy, sorry but I haven't brought any strawberry butties with me today and I'm fresh out of rotten pears."

I was surprised but this new tactic worked but only when I was still standing up. When I sat down and started fishing they swarmed around my wellies on several occasions. All I could do was get up, take a walk behind my peg and try to re-gird my loins.

Thankfully, it was only a three-hour match and we were soon packing up. I didn't even wait for the weigh-in, I threw the few fish I'd caught back in and repaired to the pub to celebrate my new found mental strength in my life long battle with wasps.

However, the truce with the old enemy didn't last long. I soon went back to my old ways with the bait box lid, knocking them for six if they came within reaching distance. Indeed, a friend of mine, Mark, can vouch for my continued hate relationship with Mr Wasp.

We were having a pleasure session on the river Trent at Repton, which I think is just about in Derbyshire. We'd chosen pegs next to each other that looked as if they would suit the stick float, but were at the same time difficult to access. The pegs were at the bottom of a steep bank and while there was enough room to stand and fish there wasn't enough space for much in the way of tackle, so a lot had to stop on top of the bank.

We'd picked well and were catching some nice chub on casters, and some good roach which were taking hemp and tares. But it was hard work and after a couple of hours I needed a break and reminded myself that this was a pleasure session, not a match. So I went back up onto the top of the bank, poured myself a cup of coffee and grabbed a bar of chocolate. I then sauntered along behind Mark, to see how he was getting on.

I guess I must have positioned myself in a wasp flight path, because as I stood there looking down at my mate, I was pestered by a succession of the horrible beasties. I had forgotten about my newly discovered calmness when it came to wasps and did my usual war dance which included flinging my arms about like a whirling dervish. At least we were in the countryside here and safe from embarrassment, when I'm approached by a wasp in the high street and do my thing, my wife always crosses the road and pretends that she doesn't know me.

Anyway, I finished my break and got back to the fishing and all was quiet until Mark stopped and climbed up the bank for his lunch.

"Mason, you're a lousy bastard," he shouted.

"Sorry Mark," I replied, as I thought I must have miss-heard him. "What was that you said?"

"You're a dirty, rotten, lousy, shit bag and should be hung up by your bollocks."

"Why?" I asked.

"Cause when you were dodging those flaming wasps you managed to dance all over my sandwiches." He held up a brown paper bag that looked like it had been trampled by a herd of Buffalo.

"Sorry Mark, I'll buy you a bag of chips on the way home." Well, what more could I do?

I think Dylan Thomas summed up the wasp perfectly. Apparently, he'd read a book all about them but said it failed to answer one simple question, why?

Tale 12: The determined angler

This is the last story in this book and I wanted to finish on a positive note, so here is a tale of determination.

We've all had those days when we know that going fishing will be a fruitless exercise. Those days when the lake is going to be frozen over or the river is in danger of bursting its banks. If you were going on your own you wouldn't bother, you'd hop back into bed and give the wife a nice surprise. But anglers are a gregarious bunch and it usually means somebody else is involved, so you look out of the window and hope and pray they won't turn up, but they always do. And even worse they are full of optimism and they're looking forward to it, as if it was a perfect summer's day.

The worst fishing I ever became involved with was the winter league; a series of team matches, which were held every month on the local canal network. I am sure they must've been organised by the tackle shop owners to keep anglers active when they'd have been better off under the duvet.

I fished several of these matches when the canal was frozen over, and must say they were all very miserable events. How anybody ever caught anything was a mystery to me, and went against everything I ever learned about the craft of angling. My father taught me to keep quiet, stay out of the skyline and approach the bank as gently as possible. Watching anglers break the ice with a house brick tied to a length of rope sort of shattered my illusion.

It was at one of these matches that this story unfolds, but before I go any further I'll give you a little insight into the world of Harry the axe-man. Harry was what I call a born again angler. For years he'd taken part in matches down the canal and won absolutely nothing. He was walking pools fodder. Every week he'd turn up, pay his money, moan about drawing the wrong peg and go home empty handed.

It was of course nothing to do with the peg, although he sometimes picked a bummer just like the rest of us. It was more to do with him as an angler, he was a chuck it and chance it merchant and used a rod a long time after the canal had been dominated by poles. His method was to cast out into the middle of the cut with curly five pound breaking strain line, and watch a float that could've saved many a ship from running aground.

He was a figure of fun to the rest of us who frequented these matches, but I must say he always took the ribbing we gave him very well. You can imagine our surprise when one day he turned up at a match with a complete new set of tackle. I don't know where Harry had got the money from, but he had the latest pole and made us all green with envy. But it didn't end there; he'd also changed his style, fine lines and ultra-sensitive floats had replaced the tackle that would previously have looked more at home in a piker's box.

With the new tackle and the new style came success and Harry soon won his first match. He now had a swagger about him: he went on to have a lot more wins and became one of the best anglers in the region.

The morning of the match in question came bright and frosty. Now, when I say frosty, I don't mean just a bit of white stuff on the lawn, I mean hoar frosty, when the trees and telephone lines are dripping with it.

"Call it off," was what most of the anglers were muttering, and I must admit that with me being a bit on the nesh side myself, it meant I was muttering it louder than everybody else. Not that I thought it would do much good, not after my failed lobbying attempts that summer to get the peg with the wasp's nest removed.

"The ice must be at least eight inches thick," one angler said.

"More like a foot," I added, not wanting to be left out.

"Soon break that," Harry said, while lifting up a full size axe, "be prepared, that's what they taught me in the scouts."

After seeing Harry's weapon, the match secretary must have thought, what the hell are we doing here on a morning like this with mad men wielding axes, because he cancelled the match. This didn't go down well with one or two of the anglers, especially Harry, but the majority were well pleased with the decision.

"I've got five pints of bloodworm and joker here, cost me a flaming fortune, what am I supposed to do with them?" he shouted loudly to a dispersing crowd. "Sod you all I'm going to fish it anyway." And that is exactly what he did.

As fate would have it I bumped into Harry the following day and asked him how he got on and this is what he said,

"Yeah, when all you sissies went home for your toast, I decided not to waste my bait and stayed on. Mind you it was touch and go; it was hard work smashing the ice even with my axe. Anyway, I decided to make a hole in the middle and fish it Eskimo style. I chopped out a square with my axe and scooped out the ice with my landing net. Then I got out my shortest whip and was all set to start, but when I got up to move my tackle box I slipped and went straight through the hole."

"Flaming heck, I bet that was cold," I said, while trying hard not to burst into laughter.

"It was flaming freezing, but the worst part was trying to get out. First I had to find the hole I'd fallen in through and then when I got my head back up through the hole in the ice I kept grasping at things trying to find something to hang on to, but everything was so slippery. Eventually, I managed to jam a rod rest in just enough to get me out. I packed my kit up in a flash and got back to the car as quick as possible, once I'd got the heater on it wasn't so bad."

"Well it looks like we made the right decision in going home, it was a day best spent in front of the fire," I said.

"Hold on a minute I haven't finished yet," he replied. "It seemed like a shame to waste that hole, so after I'd got home I changed my clothes then went back and fished it, I had thirty three gudgeon, two roach and a bullyhead."

Now that's what I call determination. It also shows passion and that's what most anglers have for this sport. It might not be as strong as Harry's, but every angler feels the pull of the water, and long may it continue.

The end

Printed in Great Britain
by Amazon